READING THE PSALMS

as an

AUBURN FAN

T. C. NOMEL

Copyright © 2011 T. C. Nomel

All rights reserved.

ISBN-10: 1463543298
ISBN-13: 978-1463543297

DEDICATION

To Mom and Dad: You will think this book a bit much, and you're right. I hope you find in its dedication my gratitude for your creating, supporting, and sometimes enduring my devotion to the Auburn Family.

CONTENTS

	Acknowledgments	i
1	Introduction	1
2	Thinking Theologically about Football?	5
3	Why the Psalms?	13
4	How Can We Say that Bammers are the Wicked?	22
5	Psalms of Lament	30
6	Psalms of Thanksgiving	42
7	Psalms of Imprecation	54
8	Those Who Contend with Us	64
9	But, What about Cam Newton?	90
Excursus	The Man Who Would Have Been Quarterback	95
10	Royal Psalms	103
11	But, What about Our Trees?	111

12	Conclusion	114
Appendix A	Video summaries	120
Appendix B	Schedules and Results	122

ACKNOWLEDGMENTS

Special thanks is due to my wonderful, beautiful, loving Wife for letting me go on and on about my ideas for this book, and for recognizing what it meant to me to write it.

1

INTRODUCTION

He appeared to have been stopped at the 45-yard line, but no whistle blew, and after some encouragement from a teammate, our freshman running back carried the ball another 32 yards down to the 23. Suddenly, the thoughts of everyone watching were moved into an entirely different realm: no more speculating about our kicker's range; no more worrying about another coin toss. A few plays later, our kicking team took the field for a 19-yard attempt, and the minds of many among the Auburn faithful drifted back to New Orleans, January 2, 1984. On that Monday night, Al Del Greco's third field goal of the game made Auburn National Champions in the eyes of some, but not all. As we waited for a field goal in Glendale, perhaps the day furthest from our minds was November 29, 2008. After 6 consecutive wins over Alabama, the Streak was put to death in gruesome fashion. The next week, Florida did what we could not, and I imagined Alabama had missed their best chance at a BCS Championship for the foreseeable future.

I was wrong. A year later, when Alabama beat Texas in Pasadena, I looked to heaven and asked *why* – why would God reward the behavior of bammers with college football's highest accomplishment? Also, given that Alabama had just gone two years with only two losses, I asked *how long* – how long until the performance of the Alabama football team no longer appeared to affirm the words and actions of bammers? These questions were inspired by their presence in the biblical Book of Psalms. There, the psalmists pose the questions of *why* and *how long* to God from very different circumstances, and, likely, in response to very different concerns. Nonetheless, I felt that the tone present in these inquiries as they appear in the Psalter expressed the same emotional substance as my lack of understanding regarding the present state of the 'bama nation,' especially as it appeared to contrast with that of the Auburn Family. With this connection in mind, I began to read the Psalter with my eyes open for further correlations between the words of the psalmists and my experience as an Auburn Fan. As the 2010 season drew near its conclusion, what I found was that the potential interactions between reading the Psalms and experiencing football as an Auburn Fan were not limited to the questions of *why* and *how long*. Accordingly, I then began to both read the Psalms with the 2008, 2009, and 2010 football seasons in mind, and also to reflect upon those seasons through the lens of the Psalms.

Please let the reader understand that I am not claiming that the primary meaning of the Psalms, nor of any book of Scripture, pertains directly to football. In evangelical Christianity, the only perspective to which I can genuinely relate, we generally hold the Bible to be directly inspired by God, in an ancient context, and we believe that the meaning conveyed in that ancient context still contains historical and theological truth, and that through it we know, in addition to the history of the ancient Israelites and the beginnings of

Christianity, the attributes of God and his redemptive work through Christ Jesus. I say all that to say that this book makes no assertions about the meaning conveyed through the Bible as it was first transmitted in its ancient context. Instead, herein is contained a reading of the Psalms that shapes my reflection upon my experience as an Auburn Fan, and I believe that it will resonate to a greater or lesser degree with many Auburn Fans.

This reflection will begin by asking some foundational questions. Firstly, why should we look at football from a theological perspective? This question will be addressed by evaluating what Scripture says about God's relationship to his creation. Secondly, we will discuss why it is the Psalms, and not some other book of the Bible, that will be referred to for perspective on the football seasons in question. This discussion will focus on the variety of genres present in the Psalter, and also the general quality of the psalmists' language. Chapter 4 will explain the place of bammers in this reading of the Psalms, and will focus on what the psalmists have to say about their enemies. Our attention will then turn more specifically to selected psalms from particular genres, namely laments, psalms of thanksgiving, and psalms of imprecation. With our examination of those psalms in mind, we will then reflect in detail upon the 2010 Auburn-Alabama game. The psalms, especially after their collection into the Psalter, functioned communally. The last Friday in November, 2010 was a special day in the life of our community, the Auburn Family, and thus it will receive special attention in this book. We have much to celebrate from 2010, but our reflection will not completely ignore everything unfortunate, and ch. 9 will deal with some of the assaults made against the Auburn family off the field. In ch. 10, however, we will return to focusing on particular psalms, this time in the genre of royal psalms.

As indicated above, I began thinking about reading the Psalms in this manner in January 2010. My thoughts about writing this book began to materialize in December 2010, but I did not make time to write it until May 2010. So these ideas have been stirring around in my head (and heart) for a while now. Still, I found new inspiration regularly as I looked back on 2008-2010 through the lens of the Psalter. It has been a fun experience to lose myself in the games and in the text while working through this project. My hope is that the reader, too, will see new meaning in their memories as they explore their own living history of Auburn Football with, at least for this moment, the Psalms as their guide.

2

THINKING THEOLOGICALLY ABOUT FOOTBALL?

    On my way home from the 2010 Alabama game I heard a caller to WJOX suggest, as an explanation for Auburn overcoming a 24-point deficit, and for Auburn's season to that point, that God was smiling on Auburn on account of Gene Chizik's faithfulness. The WJOX host responded to the caller by saying something to the effect of, *I don't think God spends time choosing sides in a football game.* Does God concern himself with the outcome of any football game or with the general success of any football program? This is a natural question for anyone who both believes in God and cares about football. It is a question that some may answer negatively if it is posed in the church house; yet, a positive response is assumed by anyone who has ever prayed regarding the outcome of a game. Of course, the game of football in its vernacular includes an acknowledgement of prayer, and, indeed, growing up Protestant, I knew Hail Mary the play long before learning it was also a prayer.

Theologically speaking, one's answer to the question of whether God concerns himself with who wins and who loses a football game should be determined by one's view of God's activity in the world. Generally, Christians believe that God created the world; and, Genesis describes God's creative work as being performed in a direct, causal, personal manner: "God said . . . and there was." God's relationship to his creation and all the events that take place within it since that initial creative activity is less clear, or, at least, it seems to be in the words and views of some.

What does the Bible have to say about God's working in the world beyond creation? Consider the following examples: Ps 147:8, "He covers the sky with clouds; he supplies the earth with rain and makes grass grow on the hills"; Lev 26:3-4, "If you follow my decrees and are careful to obey my commands, I will send you rain in its season, and the ground will yield its crops and the trees of the field their fruit."; Acts 14:17, "Yet he has not left himself without testimony: He has shown kindness by giving you rain from heaven and crops in their seasons; he provides you with plenty of food and fills your hearts with joy." These examples all pertain to God's activity with regards to nature. This category is one in which Christians generally do acknowledge the work of God; they generally do not ascribe control of the weather, nor the maintenance of natural phenomenon (e.g. grass growing as a result of rain) to any other entity. Christians do not preclude the weather from their list of appropriate prayer topics, as is evidenced in cases of drought or flood. The above example from Leviticus is particularly interesting because it presents a conditional, and, accordingly, depicts God as ready to interact with creation in response to the actions of his people. In other words, God is a hands-on manager of his creation with regards to nature.

Regarding another aspect of God's working in the world, consider the words of Joseph upon revealing his identity to his brothers in Genesis 45: "And now, do not be distressed and do not be angry with yourselves for selling me here, because it was to save lives that God sent me ahead of you . . . it was not you who sent me here, but God. He made me father to Pharaoh, lord of his entire household and ruler of all Egypt." This is an example of God intervening to set the course of history, as Joseph's rise in the house of Pharaoh led to the Israelites' sojourn into Egypt. Similar working by God is seen in the biblical accounts of the Exodus, Exile, and as well in the Israelites' return from exile.

While Christians are likely to acknowledge God's control over nature, and also to recognize his shaping the course of history, especially through deciding the outcome of major events, they sometimes are less likely to attribute to God control over the "smaller scale," everyday events in the lives of individuals (i.e., in their own lives). The everyday happenings are more often simply attributed to visible, earthly, sometimes human dynamics of cause and effect. Is this the condition to which the Bible relegates the everyday events that do not make it into history books? Ephesians 1:11-12 reads, "In him we were also chosen, having been predestined according to the plan of him who works out everything in conformity with the purpose of his will, in order that we, who were the first to hope in Christ, might be for the praise of his glory." Consider also Pr 16:9, "In his heart a man plans his course, but the LORD determines his steps." Sometimes we are hesitant to acknowledge the working of God in events in our lives and in the lives of those around us that seem relatively inconsequential. At the same time, we frequently speak of "God's plan," and we are quick to assert that "God is in control," that "God is still on his throne." We may tend to relegate God's activity in the world, in his creation, to the "big picture." Due contemplation, however, reveals that the big picture is comprised ultimately of all the details of life. Little things prove to have big impact, and little events prove to shape the character of those who go on to make great impacts. The Bible tells us that God "works out everything" – not just the major events of history, and not just the major events of one's life – "in conformity with the purpose of his will." Psalm 24 begins, "The earth is the LORD's, and everything in it, the world, and all who live in it." God's dominion is over all creation, and he does not let his dominion govern itself. God truly is in control, not just of nature and major events of history, but of everything. Job 12 speaks to the spectrum across which we may conceive of God's governance of all of his creation: "To God belong wisdom and power; counsel and understanding are his. What he tears down cannot be rebuilt; the man he imprisons cannot be released. If he holds back the waters, there is drought; if he lets them loose, they devastate the land. To him belong strength and victory; both deceived and deceiver are his. . . . He takes off the shackles put on by kings and ties a loincloth around their waist. . . . He pours contempt on nobles and disarms the mighty. He reveals the deep things of darkness and brings deep shadows into the light. He makes nations great, and destroys them; he enlarges nations, and disperses them." Job 12 addresses nature, those subjugated by kings, nobles and the mighty, nations, and also whatever hidden things might be thought unsearchably concealed. God rules over them all.

What does this have to do with football? I am not here attempting to elevate the importance of football to some place where it is there of concern to God. Instead, I am hoping to show that the teaching of the Bible is that God's management, his control and direction, of his creation is exhaustive. His reach is such that everything in his creation is sustained and guided by his providence. To say that God is unconcerned with the outcome of a football game is to say that there is something, anything, in his creation for which he does not care. That is simply not the God that we know through the Bible. Consider what a few of the most influential theologians of Christian history have said about the extent of God's activity in his creation. John Calvin interprets thusly: "For he is deemed omnipotent, not because he can indeed act, yet sometimes ceases and sits in idleness, or continues by a general impulse that order of nature which he previously appointed; but because, governing heaven and earth by his providence, he so regulates all things that nothing takes place without his deliberation."[1] John Wesley also describes a thorough involvement on the part of God in his creation: "God acts in heaven, in earth, and under the earth, throughout the whole compass of his creation; by sustaining all things, without which every thing would, in an instant, sink into its primitive nothing: by governing all, every moment superintending every thing that he has made; strongly and sweetly influencing all, and yet without destroying the liberty of his rational creatures."[2] St. Thomas Aquinas also holds this view: "God has immediate providence over everything, because He has in His intellect the types of everything, even the smallest; and whatsoever causes He assigns to certain effects, He gives them the power to produce those effects."[3]

Why is it that Christians tend to not extend the sovereignty of God to the football field? Some may truly believe that a football game is a trivial matter, that it is a contest between men, and that it is something that God

---

[1] John Calvin, *Institutes of the Christian Religion* (ed. John T. McNeil; trans. Ford Lewis Battles; 2 vols.; Louisville: Westminster John Knox Press, 1960), 1:200.

[2] John Wesley, *Sermons on Several Occasions* (2 vols.; London: T. Tegg, 1829), 1:497-498.

[3] Thomas Aquinas, *The "Summa Theologica" of St. Thomas Aquinas* (trans. Fathers of the English Dominican Province; Cincinnati: Benzinger, 1911), 311.

simply allows to play out according to earthly and human devices. For others, however, the idea of God playing a role in who wins a football game has an uncomfortable implication; it begs certain questions: if God allows us to lose, and crowns our opponent the victor, what does that say about our relationship to God, and about our relationship to God relative to that of our opponent to God? To say that God determines the outcome of a football game requires one to sometimes admit that God, for some reason, granted victory to one's opponent instead of one's own team. In other words, football fans would prefer to abstain from saying "God is on our side" so that, in defeat, they have no logical obligation to say "God is on your side." When both sides of a rivalry take this attitude, the result is a type of theological arms treaty – neither of us will claim divine allegiance, and, thus, at the outcome, neither of us will have to concede false testimony, and we can all worship the same God on Sunday. By employing this ideology, Christians choose when to emphasize God's transcendence, and when instead to emphasize his immanence.

With regards to the winner of a game, or perhaps what team has the more (or most) successful season, Christian football fans tend to only acknowledge God's transcendence. To be sure, the Bible does teach this attribute of God. Isaiah 6:1-3 reads, "In the year that King Uzziah died, I saw the Lord seated on a throne, high and exalted, and the train of his robe filled the temple. Above him were seraphs, each with six wings: With two wings they covered their faces, with two they covered their feet, and with two they were flying. And they were calling to one another: 'Holy, holy, holy is the LORD Almighty; the whole earth is full of his glory.'" Psalm 113:5-6 asks, "Who is like the LORD our God, the One who sits enthroned on high, who stoops down to look on the heavens and the earth?" In 1 Tim 6:15-16 God is described as "the blessed and only Ruler, the King of kings and Lord of lords, who alone is immortal and who lives in unapproachable light, whom no one has seen or can see." Indeed, God is high and above, and, thus, it is understandable to think that football is far too mundane to be of any concern to him. But, we cannot ignore that the Bible also teaches God's immanence. Jeremiah 23:24 reads, "'Can anyone hide in secret places so that I cannot see him?' declares the LORD. 'Do not I fill heaven and earth?' declares the LORD." Matthew 10:29-30 is often cited regarding both God's immanence and his attention to detail within his creation: "Are not two sparrows sold for a penny? Yet not one of them will fall to the ground apart from the will of your Father. And even the very hairs of your head are all numbered."

The biblical teaching depicts God not as transcendent or immanent, but as both. Consider Jeremiah 23:23, "'Am I only a God nearby,' declares the LORD, 'and not a God far away?'" Ephesians 4:6 says that there is "one God and Father of all, who is over all and through all and in all." Isaiah 57:15 also speaks to the range of God's presence and activity: "For this is what the high and lofty One says— he who lives forever, whose name is holy: 'I live in a high and holy place, but also with him who is contrite and lowly in spirit, to revive the spirit of the lowly and to revive the heart of the contrite.'" God is "above all" with the authority and power to guide the events of all creation, and he is also willing to reach as low as those "contrite and lowly in spirit." Of course, many Christian football fans understand that God is both transcendent and immanent; their deviation from the biblical teaching is that they do not allow him to be both at the same time, or, perhaps rather they themselves determine when God will be one, and when the other. For instance, Christians are quick to join with the players kneeling on the field in prayer for an injured team member. But, once play resumes, God is once again relegated high to the heavens, to leave the actual action on the field in the hands of the players and coaches.

This consideration may raise another explanation as to why Christians prefer to not attribute the outcome of games to God. It is already a vicarious experience – the players, coaches, trainers, and possibly other personnel actually participate in the game. The fans merely watch – but they do not feel that way. Fans feel that they are invested and committed enough to their program, and to the game, that they play a role in determining the outcome. Transferring the fate of the game to God removes it even further from the stands (and couches).

Let us return to the original question: Does God concern himself with the outcome of any football game or with the general success of any football program? The answer is, Yes, God concerns himself with everything in his creation. Accordingly, when the outcome of a game or season not only disappoints, but deeply disturbs us, we can look to the execution of the players, or the decisions of the coaches or administration, or the judicial rightness of the referees, but the reality is that the win or loss functioned as a part of God's will. If we feel the need to ask *why*, God is the only one, ultimately, to whom that question can be fairly posed. And, while we remember our Lord's words from Isa 55:9, "as the heavens are higher than the earth, so are my ways higher than your ways and my thoughts than your thoughts," the Psalter is the book that looks to God and asks *why*, and to the Psalms we may look when we feel the need to do the same.

3

WHY THE PSALMS?

Why the Psalms? Why is this book of Scripture, and not some other, one that an Auburn fan might read in light of 2009 and 2010? Or, rather, why is it that an Auburn fan might experience or remember 2009 and 2010 through the words of the Psalms? As mentioned in the introduction, in response to the 2009 season, I found myself wondering *why* and *how long*. Why would the Alabama football program and, more significantly, their fans be rewarded with a BCS Championship? How long would they enjoy and boast of such a prize? These questions caused me to think about the questions of *why* and *how long* as they appear in the Psalter, particularly as they are put forth by the psalmists directly to God, e.g. Ps 94:3, "How long will the wicked, O LORD, how long will the wicked be jubilant?" Psalms 94 is not the only place where the psalmist asks *how long*. It occurs ten other times, in considerably wide distribution, appearing first in Psalm 6, and lastly in Psalm 119. Accordingly, the question of *how long* is not one merely mentioned by the Psalms, but rather a recurring theme with which the book wrestles. The same is true concerning the question of *why*, which occurs 11 times, first in Psalm 10, and lastly in Psalm 88, e.g. Ps 42:9, "I say to God my Rock, 'Why have you forgotten me? Why must I go about mourning, oppressed by the enemy?'" The Psalms ask these questions in relation to the faith of the psalmists and of the people with whom the psalmists worship. They have a certain understanding of God, particularly of his righteousness and justice, and, equally as significant, they have an understanding of their relationship to God as his chosen people. The psalms that ask *why* and *how long* lift up their pleas in response to the fact that the events the psalmists are witnessing in either the life of the community or in that of an individual appear inconsistent with their understanding of who God is, who the community or the individual is in relationship to God, and the psalmists' understanding of how God administers justice in his creation.

The psalmists' understanding of the community's relationship to God is based on the covenant expressed in various ways in Deuteronomy, such as in Deuteronomy 28: "If you fully obey the LORD your God and carefully follow all his commands I give you today, the LORD your God will set you high above all the nations on earth. All these blessings will come upon you and accompany you if you obey the LORD your God: . . . The fruit of your womb will be blessed, and the crops of your land and the young of your livestock—the calves of your herds and the lambs of your flocks. . . . The LORD will grant that the enemies who rise up against you will be defeated before you. They will come at you from one direction but flee from you in seven. The LORD will send a blessing on your barns and on everything you put your hand to. The LORD your God will bless you in the land he is giving you." The psalmists refer to *covenant* 23 times. An example of how the psalms correlate their understanding of covenant to the questions of *why* and *how long* can be seen in Ps 44:15-17, "My disgrace is before me all day long, and my face is covered with shame at the taunts of those who reproach and revile me, because of the enemy, who is bent on revenge. All this happened to us, though we had not forgotten you or been false to your covenant."

As Christians, we, too, have a certain understanding of who God is. We also have a biblically instructed understanding of our relationship to him. While we know that we live in a fallen world, a world corrupted by sin where injustice abounds, we also believe that God is able to execute justice, that he is active in the world around us, and that his justice will not *en total* be reserved for the final judgment. Accordingly, when we see injustice, when we see the wicked jubilant, it is natural for us, too, to ask *why* and *how long*. The actual relationship between this phenomenon and football will be addressed in following chapters.

Another reason why the Psalms are well-suited to be read as an Auburn fan is the same reason why they are so suited to be read from a variety of perspectives other than that of ancient Israel, namely the general language of the Psalms. By general language is meant the lack of specificity regarding details which would otherwise tie the psalms indelibly to their original context. The general language of the Psalms imbue them with versatility of application that spans unrestricted spectrums of culture and time. Psalm 6 is a good example of the psalmists' use of general language. While the speaker is clearly suffering, the cause(s) of the distress are not expressly stated; accordingly, they are open to interpretation. The words of Psalm 6 might be spoken by someone suffering from any variety of illnesses, but also by anyone enduring other hardships, whether emotional distress, social persecution, or financial despair. The general language of the psalm enables it to be adapted to a variety of situations and perspectives. Psalm 6:8 mentions "all who do evil," and verse 10 refers to "my enemies," but no specific identifying information is provided. If the evildoers or enemies were identifiably named, the psalm would be connected to the original speaker's predicament in a way that would hinder its application to other situations. Its use of general language, however, allows anyone to rebuke "all who do evil" or to be confident in the eventual shame of "my enemies." This practice is ubiquitous in the Psalter. There are 93 references to "enemy" or "enemies" in the Psalter, not including other terms such as *evildoer, foe, oppressor*, and *the wicked*. Additionally, the Psalms regularly use the terms *nations* and *peoples* without specifying to just what nations or peoples they are referring.

Another way in which the Psalter lends itself to a reading from the perspective of an Auburn fan is the variety of genres of which it is comprised. In Psalms scholarship the term *genre* is often used to refer to different categories of psalms, as initially identified and grouped by Hermann Gunkel. These categories include: Hymns; Psalms of Lament or Complaint; Royal Psalms; Thanksgiving Psalms; and, Wisdom Psalms; Gunkel also designated other psalms as belonging to smaller genres or mixed types. The diversity of function exhibited by the Psalms, combined with the repeated emphasis of those functions, give the Psalter a range of emotion and expression that naturally correlates with the multi-faceted experiences of a football fan.

Psalm 29 is an example of a hymn. It begins, "Ascribe to the LORD, O mighty ones, ascribe to the LORD glory and strength. Ascribe to the LORD the glory due his name; worship the LORD in the splendor of his holiness." For a Christian, an attitude of worship is, or should be, a way of life. It is not laid to rest for football season. It is not abandoned regardless of the success, or lack thereof, of one's team. Psalm 145:2 reads, "Every day I will praise you and extol your name for ever and ever."

Psalm 80 is an example of a psalm of lament. Verses 4-6 read: "O LORD God Almighty, how long will your anger smolder against the prayers of your people? You have fed them with the bread of tears; you have made them drink tears by the bowlful. You have made us a source of contention to our neighbors, and our enemies mock us." Football fans are quick to find reason to complain. A losing season or any painful loss can result in substantial lamentation. In this book, the psalms of lament or complaint will not be read from the perspective of losing or from seeing a rival win, but rather from the perspective of disquiet that occurs when one sees injustice, when the right order of things appears to be reversed, that is, when the righteous are defeated, and the wicked victorious.

The royal psalms are generally concerned with the community's king. The king is praised, blessed, and prayed for. Of course, Christian football fans in the United States do not have a king. But, because the language and tone of the royal psalms are such that they are thought to have been performed at festivals or celebrations, their potential relationship to the experiences of football fans are clear. Great victories, great seasons, and championships inspire celebrations fit for a king.

Psalm 30 is an example of a thanksgiving psalm. It begins, "I will exalt you, O LORD, for you lifted me out of the depths and did not let my enemies gloat over me. O LORD my God, I called to you for help and you healed me. O LORD, you brought me up from the grave; you spared me from going down into the pit." Anyone who has prayed over a field goal and then watched the ball sail between the uprights should relate to the thankfulness expressed in these psalms. The life of a football fan often includes much for which to be thankful: getting tickets; making it to the game on time; safe travel; good weather – this list could extend indefinitely. When I think about the thanksgiving psalms, 2002-2007 comes to mind. The Streak was as addictive as any drug – I always felt that I could be satisfied with just one more. For me, 2005 was especially significant. We needed just one more win for a particular Alabama quarterback to finish his career without a single win against Auburn. To see him hit the turf 11 times on the day it was named Pat Dye Field was special. My thanksgiving psalm for that day is a chorus that repeats on and on.

Wisdom psalms, as their name implies, present somewhat proverbial content. Psalm 37:8-9 provides an example: "Refrain from anger and turn from wrath; do not fret—it leads only to evil. For evil men will be cut off, but those who hope in the LORD will inherit the land." Football, with regards to both the game itself and the life of the fan who follows it, has a well established corpus of conventional wisdom. "Never take points off the board" and "keep a poncho in the car" come to mind. Like the wisdom of Proverbs and Psalms, maxims such as these are often handed down through the generations. A more significant point regarding the wisdom psalms is that they are, at times and to some extent, expressions of the very faith that the psalmists question in the psalms of lament and complaint. As stated above, we will read these psalms, and others, from the perspective of an Auburn fan who believes in the God of the Bible. Still, there do exists ideas of poetic justice in the conventional wisdom of football that correlate to the faith of the wisdom psalms, e.g. "what goes around comes around."

Among the types of psalms Gunkel deems to represent smaller types, pilgrimage psalms and psalms using ancient stories of Israel especially resonate with football fans. Obviously, the word *pilgrimage* alone holds all manner of connotations for football fans. Travel is part of the lifestyle. Even for those who live relatively close to Auburn, the gameday trip involves all manner of preparation. There is food to make ready, clothing to select, and traffic to beat (ideally). The more remote the fan, the more the necessary arrangements. For some there are planes to catch and cars to rent. My favorite type of pilgrimage, when I have had the luxury to make it, involves waking up, getting ready, and then walking into town and across campus. Even without the logistical challenges, it is still to the same place, for the same reason, and it is still ceremonial in form. In 2011, Auburn fans had an extra pilgrimage to make on January 22. Regardless of the event or the ways and means needed to attend, anyone who has walked in the shade under the seats of Jordan-Hare Stadium and then emerged from a tunnel to behold the bright, sun-lit green of Pat Dye Field can appreciate the words of Ps 42:1-2, "Great is the LORD, and most worthy of praise, in the city of our God, his holy mountain. It is beautiful in its loftiness, the joy of the whole earth."

Psalms using ancient stories of Israel also correlate to a place in the life of the football fan. Psalm 105 abbreviates the history of Israel from Abraham to the water coming out of the rock in the wilderness. Football fans constantly retell their history of games and of tailgating, and even stories of watching the game at home or elsewhere. As it is for the Israelites, this living history is part of the football fan's identity, maybe even authenticity. Participating in traditions is a major component, for some, of this living history. From Tiger Walk to Toomer's Corner, even the retelling of participation in traditions is part of the endless perpetuation of what it means to be an Auburn fan, what it has meant, and what it will mean.

In summary, the correlation of reading the Psalms to the experience of a football fan, and as will be seen in following chapters, particularly the experience of an Auburn fan, is both natural and extensive. It begins with the questions of *why* and *how long*, which the psalmists address from the perspective of who God is, who the community is in relationship to God, and their understanding of God's justice. The correlation is facilitated in large part by the psalmists' use of general language, which allows the Psalms to transcend cultural, chronological, and even situational differences. The correlation is extensive – the themes of praise, lament, royalty, thanksgiving, wisdom, pilgrimage, and history seen in Gunkel's categorization of the Psalms all find a place in the life of the football fan.

The focus of this book will be a reading of Psalms from the perspective of an Auburn fan, specifically as the 2009 and 2010 seasons were experienced and are now remembered. Hopefully, this book will become a piece of the history of the extraordinary low and then the even greater high to which Auburn fans were taken by the events of these two seasons. The Psalter is more than capable of encompassing that wide range of emotion and experience in its engagement of real faith – a faith that is not afraid to claim full confidence in the ground on which it stands, even while questioning everything it sees round about.

READING THE PSALMS AS AN AUBURN FAN

4

HOW CAN WE SAY THAT BAMMERS ARE THE WICKED?

As stated earlier, for me the genesis of reading the Psalms as an Auburn fan and of experiencing and remembering 2009 and 2010 in light of the Psalms was my inclination to ask *why* and *how long* in response to Alabama's 2009 BCS championship. Of course, the fact that this led me to correlate my inquiry with Ps 94:3, which reads "How long will the wicked, O LORD, how long will the wicked be jubilant?" implies that I read "the wicked" to mean bammers. This implication may prove difficult for some to accept. At this point, I will reiterate the methodology of this book. It is not an exegesis – that is, it is not an investigation into the Book of Psalms by way of some traditional, modern, or postmodern biblical-critical approach that attempts to draw out from the text its meaning, especially with regards to its meaning in its original context nor as to its function as Scripture. Instead, this book is simply a reading of Psalms from a particular perspective, namely that of an Auburn fan, especially concerning 2009 and 2010. It is a dialogue of sorts between the text and the experience of living and remembering those two years. It is a reading of the Psalms that aims to reveal a superimposed mosaic of meaningfulness that otherwise might go unnoticed.

With this methodology in mind, let us return to the question of how one might find it appropriate to connect bammers with "the wicked." To answer this question requires an assessment of exactly what the Psalms say about the wicked. Because the psalmists use *wicked* and *enemies* without any substantive distinction (cf. Ps 17:8-9, "hide me in the shadow of your wings from the wicked who assail me, from my mortal enemies who surround me), we will include in this assessment what the psalmists say about enemies. One of the chief characteristics of the wicked in the Psalter is that they are prideful and arrogant. Consider the following examples: Ps 10:2,4, "In his arrogance the wicked man hunts down the weak . . . In his pride the wicked does not seek [God]"; Ps 123:4, "We have endured much ridicule from the proud, much contempt from the arrogant"; Ps 140:5, "Proud men have hidden a snare for me; they have spread out the cords of their net and have set traps for me along my path"; Ps 73:6, "Therefore pride is their necklace." From these examples we see that pride and arrogance are repeatedly referred to by the psalmists as traits of the wicked. Psalm 10:2,4 show those traits to be the mindset that guides how the wicked live. Psalm 73:6 is especially telling – for the wicked pride is a necklace, an ever-present adornment by which they may be identified.

Related to pride and arrogance is the verboseness of the wicked – they seem to always be speaking. Consider these examples: Ps 41:5, "My enemies say of me in malice, 'When will he die and his name perish?'"; Ps 55:2-3, "My thoughts trouble me and I am distraught at the voice of the enemy"; Ps 71:10, "For my enemies speak against me; those who wait to kill me conspire together"; Ps 102:8, "All day long my enemies taunt me; those who rail against me use my name as a curse." These examples show that another identifying characteristic of the wicked is their speech. Another way to put it is that they never shut up. Psalm 10:7 is especially clear about the significance of speech as a characteristic of the wicked: "His mouth is full of curses and lies and threats; trouble and evil are under his tongue." Psalm 64:2-3 also emphasizes the hostility of the speech of the wicked: "Hide me from the conspiracy of the wicked, from that noisy crowd of evildoers. They sharpen their tongues like swords and aim their words like deadly arrows." For the wicked, speech is a weapon. Whereas the psalmists aspires to speech of edification (cf. Ps 49:3, "My mouth will speak words of wisdom; the utterance from my heart will give understanding"), the wicked only hope by their words to oppress and destroy. Other examples directly link the pride and arrogance of the wicked to their verboseness: Ps 59:12, "For the sins of their mouths, for the words of their lips, let them be caught in their pride"; Ps 73:8, "They scoff, and speak with malice; in their arrogance they threaten oppression"; Ps 31:18, "for with pride and contempt they speak arrogantly against the righteous"; Ps 17:10, "their mouths speak with arrogance." The pride and arrogance of the wicked along with their verboseness are defining characteristics which comprise the identity of the wicked. This is further attested to by the psalmists' statements that the wicked are in need of being silenced: Ps 8:2, "From the lips of children and infants you have ordained praise because of your enemies, to silence the foe and the avenger"; Ps 143:12, "In your unfailing love, silence my enemies."

Another characteristic of the wicked delineated by the psalmists is that they hate without reason: Ps 35:19, "Let not those gloat over me who are my enemies without cause; let not those who hate me without reason maliciously wink the eye"; Ps 38:19, "Many are those who are my vigorous enemies; those who hate me without reason are numerous." The psalmists make it clear that there is no just cause for the enmity of the wicked; there is no wrong by the psalmists that they are desiring to repay.

Unfortunately, the psalmists also describe the wicked as being great in number: Ps 25:19, "See how my enemies have increased and how fiercely they hate me!"; Ps 69:4, "Those who hate me without reason outnumber the hairs of my head; many are my enemies without cause, those who seek to destroy me." The large numbers of the wicked are attested to both by these examples and also simply by the pervasiveness of enemies throughout the Psalter.

Before examining the correlation of the traits and characteristics of the wicked to bammers, it is appropriate to explain just what/who we mean by the term. Over the years I have contemplated a few different working definitions of *bammer*. Some consider anyone who declares himself to be an Alabama football fan to be a bammer. I have generally felt uncomfortable with such an all-encompassing classification, as I prefer to reserve the term as a title for those who embody some quintessential quality comprised of the most negative aspects of association with the Alabama football program. I especially feel that a narrower categorization is needed when examining the relationship of bammers to the enemies of the psalmists. The question, of course, remains – what is the quintessential quality, the exhibition of which makes one a bammer? The first answer to this question that I considered was that a bammer is anyone who accepts and promotes the legitimacy of Alabama's late-modern claim of 13 national championships. My preliminary research, however, failed to produce an example of an Alabama fan who does not meet this criterion. Of course, not finding an Alabama fan who does not meet a proposed criterion for being a bammer supports the proposal that all Alabama fans are bammers.

Nonetheless, out of my conviction that it is still unfair to group all Alabama fans with those who represent the worst aspects of the bama nation, I continued to analyze other possible definitions. The second definition I considered was that a bammer was an Alabama fan who never attended the University of Alabama at Tuscaloosa. This criterion seemed promising because it did seem to emphasize a distinction between bammers and Auburn fans, as it is less common to encounter a fanatic Auburn supporter who never attended Auburn University. But, whereas the former definition was too encompassing, this one proved too narrow. The reality is that there are certainly many Alabama fans who represent the negative elements of the bama nation who did in fact attend or even earn a degree from UAT. At the same time, this definition creates an unfair implication against those who never attended Auburn who do, in fact, represent the true Spirit of the Auburn Family. Ultimately, I settled on a definition of *bammer* once I came to realize the fundamental distinction between the ideologies promoted by the two schools.

On one side, UAT identifies with the concept of "rightful place," that is, the assumption that the bama nation is somehow deserving of respect, and even success, not as a result of their actions, but necessarily as a result of their identity as the bama nation. This ideology has surfaced most visibly in recent instances when Alabama has had success on the football field after a period of falling short of expectations. Whenever Alabama has had successful seasons, or even Septembers, they have not spoken simply of once again reaching a previously enjoyed level of success, but rather of returning to their "rightful place." This begs the question: why is it their rightful place? How is it that having won several games under Paul Bryant's manipulation of a less regulated collegiate football structure causes bammers to be owed something, to be entitled to celebration? There is, of course, no reasonable positive response to this question. While this sense of entitlement is primarily promoted by the football program, it certainly appears to have infected the University of Alabama at Tuscaloosa with regards to their general persona, and, all the more so, it has been adopted by Alabama fans.

The Alabama ideology of "rightful place" is contrasted by the Auburn Family's belief in the Auburn Creed, which contradicts the bammers' sense of entitlement in its first lines: "I believe that this is a practical world and that I can count only on what I earn. Therefore, I believe in work, hard work."[4] Whereas Alabama decided in the 1980s to begin celebrating national championships they had never before recognized, Auburn made the decision in the early 2000s to place a renewed emphasis on the Auburn Creed, and have thereby successfully galvanized the place of the Creed in how the Auburn Family conceives of its own identity. Of course, the renewed emphasis did not create the Auburn family's belief "in these things,"[5] but rather only brought about a more publicly visible expression thereof. In light of this distinction between the ideologies associated with the two institutions, a satisfactory definition of *bammer* may be enunciated. A *bammer* is anyone who by their words and actions affirms the validity of the "rightful place" mindset.

Having defined the term *bammer*, our next task is to show the correlation between bammers and the enemies of the psalmists. Of course, for any Auburn fan who has had any substantial interaction with bammers, the correlation, in light of the survey above, is obvious. But, for the benefit of those otherwise so fortunate, let us look at each characteristic. The

---

[4] George Petrie, "The Auburn Creed," n.p. [cited 05/11/2011]. Online: http://www.auburn.edu/main/auburn_creed.html.

[5] Petrie, "The Auburn Creed," n.p.

first identifier of the psalmists' enemies observed above was that they are prideful and arrogant. *Pride*, of course, can be a positive term. To take pride in one's work is a good thing. This is not the type of pride in which bammers specialize. Their kind of pride is that which we might describe using another word employed at times by the psalmists – "haughty" (cf. Ps 101:5). Bammers exhibit a particular nuance of pride – they take pride in being proud for no reason. In some regard, this phenomenon traces back to the words of Paul Bryant, "I ain't never been nothin' but a winner." The type of pride being discussed here was likely not intended in the words of Bryant, but his worshippers have imparted to them such a connotation. It is as if bammers consider themselves to be winners by virtue of Bryant's own designation of himself as such. And in this they take great pride.

The next characteristic of the psalmists' enemies is their verboseness. Bammer never quit talking. They have an answer for everything. They have a criticism for anyone who does not bow at their feet.

The next trait of the wicked is that they hate without reason. This has been experienced by any Auburn fan, oftentimes when meeting a bammer for the first time. As soon as a bammer learns that someone is an Auburn fan, they open their mouth and let a few arrows fly. They need not know anything else about the Auburn fan – they do not wait to judge the Auburn fan's words or actions – they know all that they need to know.

Finally, the enemies of the psalmists are many. Anyone who has lived in Birmingham can relate to bammers outnumbering the hairs of one's head. One reason for this is that the "rightful place," entitlement mindset is attractive to many who are uneducated. There is not a correspondingly large contingent of non-affiliated Auburn fans who are attracted to the Auburn Creed because oftentimes people who have no connection to either institution, but find the Creed more attractive than "rightful place," have other things in life to care about over and against a rivalry between two schools, neither of which they attended. With regards to the psalmists' characterization of their enemies as prideful and arrogant, verbose, hateful, and innumerable, a clear correlation with bammers exists. The Hebrew word אֹיְבַי, translated "my enemies," is a participle, meaning it is a noun form of a verb (אָיַב), in this case with a first-person, singular pronominal suffix, so that it literally means "the ones being hostile to me." The significance of this is that the psalmists do not proactively designate anyone as their enemy. Instead, they use a term describing action on the part of others in response to that action. Likewise, I am not claiming that the psalms indicate bammers as the wicked or the enemy, but rather that bammers, by their words and actions, liken themselves unto the Psalm's characterization of enemies.

In conclusion, it is the pride and arrogance, verboseness, hatefulness, and ubiquity of bammers that caused me to ask *why* and *how long* in response to Alabama's 2009 BCS championship, and it is their behavior that establishes their correlation to the wicked and the enemies in the Psalter. This correlation determines their role in my reading of the Psalms as an Auburn fan.

5

PSALMS OF LAMENT

Psalms of complaint comprise a major component of the Psalter. Gunkel classifies 46 of the 150 psalms as either communal or individual complaints. Complaining to God is not something we generally think of as a commendable function within the Christian faith. This may be in part because most Christians living in America do not experience the type of threats endured by the psalmists. Nonetheless, lament language makes up a sizable portion of the one book of the Bible that is sometimes called not just the Word of God, but also words to God. To exclude psalms of complaint from our prayers is to deny something of the omniscience of God. We act as though by not verbalizing our confusion over negative experiences that it will be effectively hidden from God. We also deny our own humanity. We are not in control, and it is only human to complain to the One who is when we see injustice in his creation. With regards to recent history, it is not just Alabama's 2009 BCS championship that comes to mind when I read the psalms of complaint. Our season of lament really started in 2008, a year in which a mid-season loss to Vanderbilt began a winless streak interrupted only by an unimpressive performance against Tennessee-Martin - a year ended by a 36-0 loss to Alabama that completed an undefeated regular season for the Tied.[6] More significantly, that loss was the end of the Streak, the conclusion of a time of prosperity. Another reason for lament is just how close we came in 2009 to ruining Alabama's season. Our coaches prepared a near-perfect game plan, and our players played their hearts out. They laid their guts on the line.[7] Yet another thing to lament from that era is Alabama's first Heisman trophy, despite our shutting down their running back at season's end. Previously, that had been a claim only Auburn could make in the rivalry. Their 2009 Heisman brought the Tied program within only one of the number of Heismans won by Auburn.[8] The 2008-2009 period provided plenty over which to lament. The fact that almost a third of the Psalter is comprised of laments shows the potential efficacy of the Psalms to provide shape to our understanding and remembering the darker moments of those years. Now we will focus our attention on two particular psalms of lament in order to see what insight they may provide to our reflection upon 2008-2009.

Psalm 38

A psalm of David. A petition.

1 O LORD, do not rebuke me in your anger
 or discipline me in your wrath.
2 For your arrows have pierced me,
 and your hand has come down upon me.

---

[6] This spelling of UAT's nickname makes more sense than "Tide" because it reflects the origin of the name: the bammers' excitement over managing a tie against Auburn in 1907 ("We tied!").

[7] see http://www.youtube.com/watch?v=-EjuEc2QBw8

[8] At the time.

³ Because of your wrath there is no health in my body;
   my bones have no soundness because of my sin.
⁴ My guilt has overwhelmed me
   like a burden too heavy to bear.

⁵ My wounds fester and are loathsome
   because of my sinful folly.
⁶ I am bowed down and brought very low;
   all day long I go about mourning.
⁷ My back is filled with searing pain;
   there is no health in my body.
⁸ I am feeble and utterly crushed;
   I groan in anguish of heart.

⁹ All my longings lie open before you, O Lord;
   my sighing is not hidden from you.
¹⁰ My heart pounds, my strength fails me;
   even the light has gone from my eyes.
¹¹ My friends and companions avoid me because of my wounds;
   my neighbors stay far away.
¹² Those who seek my life set their traps,
   those who would harm me talk of my ruin;
   all day long they plot deception.

¹³ I am like a deaf man, who cannot hear,
   like a mute, who cannot open his mouth;
¹⁴ I have become like a man who does not hear,
   whose mouth can offer no reply.
¹⁵ I wait for you, O LORD;
   you will answer, O Lord my God.
¹⁶ For I said, "Do not let them gloat
   or exalt themselves over me when my foot slips."

¹⁷ For I am about to fall,
   and my pain is ever with me.

[18] I confess my iniquity;
 I am troubled by my sin.
[19] Many are those who are my vigorous enemies;
 those who hate me without reason are numerous.
[20] Those who repay my good with evil
 slander me when I pursue what is good.

[21] O LORD, do not forsake me;
 be not far from me, O my God.
[22] Come quickly to help me,
 O Lord my Savior.

(vv. 1-4) The psalm begins with something of an invocation. It may be read as asking God to hear the complaint with patience, rather than responding to even the psalmist's daring to speak with anger. In vv. 2 and 3a it is made clear that the source of the speaker's distress is God. Likewise, in acknowledging God's sovereignty over all events, our response to the events of 2008 and 2009 is to look not to earthly actors or causes for an explanation, but to God. Verses 3b and 4 indicate that the speaker's weakness has resulted from his own sin. While we may not see Alabama's 2009 BCS championship as due punishment for some sin on the part of the Auburn Family, we must nonetheless recognize that we all are guilty of sin (cf. Rom 3:23). The world in which we live is corrupted by the presence of sin, and one result of that is injustice. Psalm 38 may sound like a confession of a particular sin. If that is the case, we can still relate to the fact that sin has consequences - painful ones; and, furthermore, it is not incorrect for us to conceive of a causal relationship between injustice and sin in a general sense, including our own sin. Also in vv. 2-4 are an idea we can relate to more directly – the severity of the anguish. The arrows of 2008 and 2009 were indeed sharp enough to pierce. Constant reminders of the injury rid all health from the body and all reliability from the bones. The burden was heavy, and it sometimes seemed like it simply could not be borne.

(vv 5-8) The next section of the psalm describes the anguish more graphically, still. The long stretch from January to September, really from early December to September, provided no means by which to dress the wounds, leaving them plenty of time to fester. One might argue that the recruiting success of 2009-2010 eased the pain. While seeing the energy of Chizik and Trooper, knowing it represented the commitment of the entire staff, and the results it produced certainly provided a bright spot, it could not (yet) undo the damage. In our lowest moments, we could relate to the bowing down and mourning of the psalmist. Again, the weight of the burden took its toll on one's back. The depths of seemingly hopelessness expressed in v. 8 bring to mind the feeling of witnessing something that, in all honesty, I had thought I may never see again in my lifetime. It crushed me, at least for a moment, and the anguish was indeed located in my heart.

(vv.9-10) Like the psalmist, our despair was laid out before the eyes of the Lord. Nothing escapes his notice. It would be illogical not to raise a complaint to him, for he already knows our anguish, confusion, and disbelief in full. He knows our hearts. Verse 10 continues the emphasis on the physical manifestation of grief. As will be clear later in the psalm, the speaker's distress is not from conventional bodily illness, but rather he or she is suffering the effects of a disease from without that wrecks his soul to the point that health departs from his body.

(v. 11) Verse 11, thankfully, expresses something to which members of the Auburn Family cannot relate. As a healthy family should, we drew closer in our time of tragedy. War Eagle and references to the Creed filled our speech to one another in a way perhaps never before seen. We bonded in commiseration; so, too, did we join our hearts and minds in the hope for better days to come. We did not stay far away from our Auburn Family, but instead traveled great distances to be together, to celebrate all things Auburn, the most visible such gathering being A-Day.

(v. 12-16) Here is where it becomes clear that the psalmist is not suffering ultimately from physical illness. Neither does he or she attribute his or her distress solely to punishment for sin. Instead, the agents of the misery are "Those who seek my life." They exhibit consistency with one of the characteristics of the enemies discussed above in that they speak. The deception plotted by bammers was the assertion that their "rightful place" ideology had been unequivocally validated by winning a BCS championship. In vv. 13-14 the psalmist describes his or her inability to combat the onslaught of the enemies on account that he or she is too weak. We, too, struggled to offer a reply. How were we to understand what we were experiencing? Like the psalmist, we could only wait for an answer from God. We knew that somehow it was in his will to allow these things to happen; in response we could only hope he would provide some explanation. Our enemies were already exalting themselves over us, and all we could do was wait for God to bring their gloating to an end.

(vv. 17-18) Verse 17 emphasizes the constancy of the pain. Whether at work, school, church, or just driving down the road, for anyone living in the state of Alabama, declarations of the 2009 BCS championship were rarely out of sight. Beyond that, whenever I closed my eyes, I could see various plays from the 2009 Alabama game, knowing that had any one of them gone the other way, the questions of *why* and *how long* would have never entered my mind. Verse 18 again brings attention to the speaker's sin, but not in a way that points to it as the root of the distress, as evidenced by the fact that the psalmist immediately returns in the next two verses to the aggression of the enemies. Instead, it is simply included as a confession that belongs in any complaint to God – an acknowledgment that the speaker is not without sin, and thus cannot completely cast all responsibility away from himself or herself.

(vv. 19-20) Here the psalmist laments the ubiquity, hatefulness, and vigor of the enemies. They are again depicted as speaking in that they slander. The senselessness of the enemies' antagonism is clearly a significant element of what makes their attacks so depressing.

(vv. 21-22) Psalm 38 closes with an appeal to God to draw near and to provide help. This is all one can do in response to such severe distress. We were helpless to right the wrongs of 2008-2009. Though it was only natural to ask the questions *why* and *how long*, to dwell on them would have been fruitless. As asking God to quickly intervene with help is an appropriate conclusion to Psalm 38, so it also is to lamenting our lack of understanding concerning 2008-2009.

Psalm 42

For the director of music. A *maskil* of the Sons of Korah.

[1] As the deer pants for streams of water,
   so my soul pants for you, O God.
[2] My soul thirsts for God, for the living God.
   When can I go and meet with God?
[3] My tears have been my food
   day and night,
while men say to me all day long,
   "Where is your God?"
[4] These things I remember
   as I pour out my soul:
how I used to go with the multitude,
   leading the procession to the house of God,

with shouts of joy and thanksgiving
   among the festive throng.

5 Why are you downcast, O my soul?
   Why so disturbed within me?
Put your hope in God,
   for I will yet praise him,
   my Savior and 6 my God.

My soul is downcast within me;
   therefore I will remember you
from the land of the Jordan,
   the heights of Hermon—from Mount Mizar.
7 Deep calls to deep
   in the roar of your waterfalls;
all your waves and breakers
   have swept over me.

8 By day the LORD directs his love,
   at night his song is with me—
   a prayer to the God of my life.

9 I say to God my Rock,
   "Why have you forgotten me?
Why must I go about mourning,
   oppressed by the enemy?"
10 My bones suffer mortal agony
   as my foes taunt me,
saying to me all day long,
   "Where is your God?"

11 Why are you downcast, O my soul?
   Why so disturbed within me?
Put your hope in God,
   for I will yet praise him,
   my Savior and my God.

(vv. 1-2) Here the psalmist describes an unquenched thirst for God. The question of *how long* has been nuanced into 'how long until I can meet with God?' This question indicates that God seems to be missing, and the psalmist knows not how long until his return.

(v. 3) In the absence of all the good things that result from God's presence, the psalmist is left to a diet of his or her own tears, a meal made all the more enjoyable by the taunts of those round about.

(v. 4) Verse 4 indicates that pleasant memories now only make things worse, as the psalmist is haunted by fellowship, joy, and festivity he or she knew in the past. This brings to mind 2002-2007, years that were not perfect by any criteria, but, at least there was no threat of bammers' behavior being rewarded by a BCS championship, or even a state championship.

(v. 5) These lines are the critical turning point in the psalm. Here the speaker turns the question of *why* back on himself. Instead of asking why God would bestow upon the wicked blessings normally reserved for the righteous, the psalmist asks himself why he should succumb to depression as if he had no reason for hope. The psalmist goes on to encourage himself to place his hope in God and to praise God.

(v. 6) Just as v. 5 reversed the direction for the question *why*, so does v. 6 reverse the function of remembering. Instead of being haunted by visions of joy in the past, here the psalmist cites his or her memory of God as therapy for a downcast soul, even as God's "waves and breakers" sweep over him. As we endured the ongoing celebration of Alabama's 2009 BCS championship, we would have been wise to remember that God was still in control, and that the question "Where is your God?" would not remain forever unanswered.

(v. 8) Verse 8 is like a miniature hymn of praise inserted within the complaint. It is the reality check to which vv. 5-7 have been pointing. God is never truly absent. He is always omnipresent and actively working in his creation. The fact that he appeared to have withdrawn his presence says more about our inability to see him than it does about his actual place.

(v. 9-10) In verse 9 the psalmist addresses God. In a way, this is putting faith into action. The psalmist is expressing his belief that God is able to act and to reverse the psalmist's fortune. Here again the psalmist employs questions of *why*. He also attests to the physical manifestation of his agony and the enemies' defining characteristic of verboseness. Verse 10 includes the second quotation in this psalm of the enemies asking "Where is your God?" By repeating this question, the psalm sheds light on the theology of the enemies. Firstly, it shows that they understand their oppression of the psalmist to constitute apparent absence of God, i.e. they realize that the psalmist's perception of God is challenged by the enemies' successful assaults against the psalmist. Secondly, it also shows that the enemies are unaware of the reason for hope the psalmist still has – they do not realize that their continued taunting will ultimately be silenced.

(v. 11) Psalm 42 concludes by repeating v. 5. This refrain emphasizes that the psalmist would be foolish to concede final defeat as if he or she had no reason for hope of deliverance.

From this reading of Psalms 38 and 42 we see the varied approach of the psalmists when presenting complaints to God. There is a general sense of helplessness and a corresponding dependence upon God. The impact of the psalmist's distress upon his physical health is emphasized, and the enemies are characterized in ways consistent with their traits described in other psalms. Psalm 38 concludes by crying to God for help, and Psalm 42 concludes by repeating the speaker's self-chastisement for failing to exhibit the hope that results from remembering God. As Auburn fans, we see in the laments expressed every bit of the pain and confusion we experienced in 2008 and 2009. As we remember those years, if we keep in mind the psalms of lament, we realize that part of the proper response to injustice is to look to heaven and ask *why*, even while remembering that God is fully aware of our confusion and that we always have hope because of who God is.

Awaiting the kickoff of the Gene Chizik era, we hoped to be leaving our laments in the past.

6

PSALMS OF THANKSGIVING

In the Psalter, the other side of lament is thanksgiving. Often thanksgiving psalms praise God for delivering the psalmists and/or the community from just the sort of distress that was referred to in the laments. We would be apostate to see in the laments our depression over undesirable events in the past without also recognizing the place of thanksgiving in our deliverance from the state caused by such events. In the thanksgiving psalms a direct correlation is made between the psalmists having cried out to God for help and God stepping in to provide salvation (e.g. Ps 34:4, "I sought the LORD, and he answered me; he delivered me from all my fears"; Ps 138:3, "When I called, you answered me; you made me bold and stouthearted"). Accordingly, the thanksgiving psalms entail certain implications about the attributes of God: He is a God who listens, who remembers, who shows mercy. Just as the psalms of lament graphically describe the extent of the psalmists' suffering, so do the thanksgiving psalms illustrate the goodness of God's blessing with rich imagery (cf. Ps 92:10, "You have exalted my horn like that of a wild ox; fine oils have been poured upon me"). In reading psalms of thanksgiving, it is natural for us to think of the 2010 season. In this chapter, we will restrict our contemplation to the first 11 games of the season, looking back on them specifically in light of Psalms 30, 92 and 116.

Psalm 30

A psalm. A song. For the dedication of the temple. Of David.

[1] I will exalt you, O LORD,
   for you lifted me out of the depths
   and did not let my enemies gloat over me.
[2] O LORD my God, I called to you for help
   and you healed me.
[3] O LORD, you brought me up from the grave;
   you spared me from going down into the pit.

[4] Sing to the LORD, you saints of his;
   praise his holy name.
[5] For his anger lasts only a moment,
   but his favor lasts a lifetime;
weeping may remain for a night,
   but rejoicing comes in the morning.

[6] When I felt secure, I said,
   "I will never be shaken."
[7] O LORD, when you favored me,
   you made my mountain stand firm;
but when you hid your face,
   I was dismayed.

[8] To you, O LORD, I called;
   to the Lord I cried for mercy:
[9] "What gain is there in my destruction,
   in my going down into the pit?
Will the dust praise you?

Will it proclaim your faithfulness?
¹⁰ Hear, O LORD, and be merciful to me;
O LORD, be my help."

¹¹ You turned my wailing into dancing;
you removed my sackcloth and clothed me with joy,
¹² that my heart may sing to you and not be silent.
O LORD my God, I will give you thanks forever.

(vv. 1-3) Psalm 30 gets right to the point, praising the Lord for lifting the psalmist out of the depths. The first 11 games of the 2010 season certainly lifted Auburn fans from the depths of the miserable 2008 season and the disappointments from the latter half of the 2009 season. The fact that we had clinched the SEC Western Division prior to playing Alabama provided serious rebuttal to the previous two years of gloating by our enemies. For those who had looked to heaven and asked *why* and *how long*, God's help was now at hand, and some degree of healing already administered. Each of the first three games of the 2010 season seemed to indicate that we would surely lose the next, but, instead, the Lord brought us up from the grave, and spared us from the pit to which a slow start might have led.

(vv. 4-5) As it became clear that our team would be a conference, and potentially a national, contender, our song returned to our mouths. Once we were again enjoying success, 2008, a season that could not end soon enough, became only a moment, and our present joy connected us to great seasons of the past, reminding us of God's favor throughout our lifetime. The nights of 2008 and 2009 were dark, and weeping was indeed a seemingly entrenched guest, but 2010 brought a bright morning.

(vv. 6-7) Verses 6-7 again bring to mind 2002-2007. There were moments when it was easy to think that we had been lifted up to a height from which we could not be toppled. Our mountain appeared to be firmly established with 7 flags flying around its highest point.[9] Unfortunately, 2008 proved that we had not faced grief for the last time. The losses of that year, and the ways we managed to lose games, along with the other lamentable events described in the previous chapter made it seem as though God had hidden his face, that he had looked away from us, leaving our fate in the hands of those who hated us without reason.

(vv. 8-10) In our dire straits, all we could do was plead to the Lord for mercy. Those facing destruction are often prone to bargain with God, and here the psalmist attempts the only line of reasoning that seems suitable when addressing the sovereign King of the Universe: *if I am destroyed, how can I praise you?* The psalmist acknowledges that he or she is not deserving of God's help for any reason – the request is only that God be merciful for mercy's sake.

(vv. 11-12) The conclusion of Psalm 30 shows that God's response results in a complete reversal of the psalmist's situation. In 2010, our wailing was indeed turned to dancing, just as our offense danced around defenders to astronomical production. Not only could we not be silent, but now the entire nation was singing our praises. It had become clear that we had the best team in the country, and it was nice to again hear Auburn discussed on the national level. God had given us a reminder that he is due praise forever.

---

[9] Six for each win over UAT plus a seventh for the 2004 SEC Championship.

T. C. NOMEL

Psalm 92

A psalm. A song. For the Sabbath day.

[1] It is good to praise the LORD
   and make music to your name, O Most High,
[2] to proclaim your love in the morning
   and your faithfulness at night,
[3] to the music of the ten-stringed lyre
   and the melody of the harp.

[4] For you make me glad by your deeds, O LORD;
   I sing for joy at the works of your hands.
[5] How great are your works, O LORD,
   how profound your thoughts!
[6] The senseless man does not know,
   fools do not understand,
[7] that though the wicked spring up like grass
   and all evildoers flourish,
they will be forever destroyed.

[8] But you, O LORD, are exalted forever.

[9] For surely your enemies, O LORD,
   surely your enemies will perish;
   all evildoers will be scattered.
[10] You have exalted my horn like that of a wild ox;
   fine oils have been poured upon me.
[11] My eyes have seen the defeat of my adversaries;
   my ears have heard the rout of my wicked foes.

[12] The righteous will flourish like a palm tree,
   they will grow like a cedar of Lebanon;
[13] planted in the house of the LORD,
   they will flourish in the courts of our God.
[14] They will still bear fruit in old age,

they will stay fresh and green,
¹⁵ proclaiming, "The LORD is upright;
he is my Rock, and there is no wickedness in him."

(vv. 1-3) Psalm 92 begins with a general statement about the goodness of praising the Lord. In 2010, our reasons to praise were never out of mind; they brightened our eyes every morning, and sweetened our dreams every night. Each Saturday added a new instrument to the symphony our coaches and players were composing.

(vv. 4-7) The 2010 season indeed showed the profundity of the thoughts of the Lord. In the aftermath of 2008 and even 2009, no one could have imagined how the works of God's hands would bring everything together in the way that they did. An idiot does not see the handiwork of God in events such as this. They are instead attributed to mere men, or to luck, chance, etc.. Also, the simpleminded do not know that the success of the wicked is fleeting. In v. 7, the psalmist acknowledges that "the wicked spring up" and "evildoers flourish." For some reason, in the sin-corrupted world of the present, this is part of God's plan. Nonetheless, it is subject to his will, and, in the end, "they will be forever destroyed."

(v. 8) In contrast to evildoers and the wicked, the Lord will be, as he has been, exalted forever. The years 2008 and 2009 presented realities that we did not understand; 2010 brought higher joy than we had ever known; no one but God knows what the future holds. Regardless, the Lord has been, is, and will be exalted forever.

(vv. 9-11) These lines of Psalm 92 require especially careful treatment. At issue here are both the enemies of the Lord and those of the psalmist. We have already discussed how bammers liken themselves unto the enemies of the psalmists. But, I will not judge them to the point of calling them the enemies of the Lord. Of course, some bammers are enemies of the Lord, as are some Auburn fans. Unfortunately, the enemies of the Lord are a widely reaching populace. To define the enemies of the Lord is beyond the scope of this work. That is such a delicate and theologically complex question that I will not even offer the simplest of answers to it. There is another issue regarding the enemies that must be addressed here. We have established that bammers, by their words and actions, align themselves with the enemies of the psalmists. Because this chapter is about the first 11 games of the 2010 season, it is important to state that when we encounter the psalmist's enemies in vv. 9-11 we do not see in them the fans of other programs. While fans of LSU, Georgia, Ole Miss, etc. may at times live out a similar ideology as that of bammers, no one else is so delusionally committed to their own concept of self-majesty as to constitute connecting themselves to the enemies of the psalmists. So when we talk about the defeat and rout of our enemies in the first 11 games of the 2010 season, we are still talking about beating bammers. This is the case because every win by Auburn brings disappointment to bammers, and, more significantly, every win by Auburn affirms the validity of the Creed, which opposes all things in which bammers take pride.

(vv. 12-15) The closing section of Psalm 92 describes the blessed position of the righteous. As the righteous will bear fruit even in old age, so will the triumphs of the 2010 season gladden and inspire Auburn fans until the end of the present age.

Psalm 116

[1] I love the LORD, for he heard my voice;
   he heard my cry for mercy.
[2] Because he turned his ear to me,
   I will call on him as long as I live.

³ The cords of death entangled me,
  the anguish of the grave came upon me;
  I was overcome by trouble and sorrow.
⁴ Then I called on the name of the LORD:
  "O LORD, save me!"

⁵ The LORD is gracious and righteous;
  our God is full of compassion.
⁶ The LORD protects the simplehearted;
  when I was in great need, he saved me.

⁷ Be at rest once more, O my soul,
  for the LORD has been good to you.

⁸ For you, O LORD, have delivered my soul from death,
  my eyes from tears,
  my feet from stumbling,
⁹ that I may walk before the LORD
  in the land of the living.
¹⁰ I believed; therefore I said,
  "I am greatly afflicted."
¹¹ And in my dismay I said,
  "All men are liars."

¹² How can I repay the LORD
  for all his goodness to me?
¹³ I will lift up the cup of salvation
  and call on the name of the LORD.
¹⁴ I will fulfill my vows to the LORD
  in the presence of all his people.

¹⁵ Precious in the sight of the LORD
  is the death of his saints.
¹⁶ O LORD, truly I am your servant;
  I am your servant, the son of your maidservant;
  you have freed me from my chains.

¹⁷ I will sacrifice a thank offering to you
and call on the name of the LORD.
¹⁸ I will fulfill my vows to the LORD
in the presence of all his people,
¹⁹ in the courts of the house of the LORD—
in your midst, O Jerusalem.

Praise the LORD.

(vv. 1-2) The beginning of Psalm 116 affirms the correlation between the psalmist's cry for help and the Lord responding in mercy. As was clear from the desperation described in the laments, nothing remained for the psalmist to do in effort to produce his own deliverance. From a place of complete vulnerability, he sends his distress call to God.

(vv. 3-4) Here the psalmist illustrates just how near to death the oppression of his enemies had brought him. He felt the cords of death making their way, twisting around his legs in preparation to drag him to *Sheol*. He was already feeling the mental condition of being destroyed. In v. 4 the psalmist responds to this predicament in the only way that has any hope of success – he calls on the name on the Lord.

(vv. 5-6) The psalmist praises God's attributes of graciousness and righteousness. He testifies to God's intervention in the psalmist's time of great need.

(v. 7) Verse 7 is a critical point in Psalm 116. In a sense, this is where the theology of the psalm brings it all back home, where it keeps it real. The words remind us of certain lines from a particular lament psalm: "Why are you downcast, O my soul? Why so disturbed within me?" (Ps 42:5). When in the state of lament, the psalmist's soul was in such feeble condition that the psalmist was forced to chastise his own lack of faith. But, after deliverance, in this hymn of thanksgiving, we hear a much different internal conversation,

"Be at rest once more, O my soul, for the LORD has been good to you."

(vv. 8-11) The psalmist again contrasts the previous devastation with the blessing of having been delivered by the Lord. "All men are liars," and thus worthless for making good on any promise to deliver from affliction.

(vv. 12-14) Verse 12 asks how the speaker can repay all the goodness from the Lord. Of course, the answer is that we by no means have the capacity to do so. The psalmist concludes that he will do what he can, performing acts of worship and fulfilling his vows. We do not have the practice of vow making as the psalmist did. Nonetheless, our deliverance begs the question – how should we respond to God delivering us from 2008 and 2009 into the blessing of 2010? The answer is simple, that being just to do what God wants us to do all the time. Consider John 14:15, "If you love me, you will obey what I command" and Mark 12:29-31, "'The most important one,' answered Jesus, 'is this: 'Hear, O Israel, the Lord our God, the Lord is one. Love the Lord your God with all your heart and with all your soul and with all your mind and with all your strength.' The second is this: 'Love your neighbor as yourself.' There is no commandment greater than these."

(vv. 15-19) The last section of Psalm 116 reiterates the psalmist's determination to respond to God's mercy appropriately. We, too, should be so concerned not to act as though our deliverance was something we deserved, or, even worse, something we brought about by our own devices.

What do the thanksgiving psalms teach us? Expressing thanks, like lamenting, is an act of faith. In doing so we should remember what the connection between calling out to God and being delivered by him tells us about God: he is mindful, gracious, and righteous. In giving thanks to God we should also acknowledge that God alone is capable of providing salvation. We cry out to God for deliverance, not believing that we for some reason have a right to be saved, but only in knowing him to be merciful, and we appeal to his mercy. While God needs nothing from us, and we can in no way repay his goodness, we should desire to respond to God's providence in gratitude, manifested in our love for him and for each other.

The 2010 season, even if we just think about the first 11 games, was special. It is special even among its contemporaries, 1993 and 2004. In 1993, the momentum gathered slowly but surely. Every game had the potential to be a trap, and by mid-season each of our opponents viewed their game with us as a chance to make their season. Still, to the observant, the undeniability of that team was apparent fairly early. The 2004 team needed a few heroic moments to prevail against LSU early in the season, but soon after that our attention was on other teams more than our own with regards to how our season would end. The 2010 season had a unique feel. It started on frighteningly shaky legs. Even as our team's confidence developed before our eyes, it was hard not to wonder, *when is it going to end*. At times it seemed too wild a ride for us to possibly hold on the whole way. The fact that we did hang on attests to how great are our reasons to sing songs of thanksgiving, to praise God for showing us mercy, for delivering us, for lifting us up above our enemy.

We waited in line about 2 hours after A-Day 2010 for Coach Chizik's autograph. I thanked him. He thanked me for attending the game, and I feel like he meant it.

7

PSALMS OF IMPRECATION

On November 13, 2010, Auburn overcame a 1st quarter 14 point deficit to defeat Georgia 49-31. Though it had seemed to be our official policy all season to spot our opponents at least that large a lead, the Georgia game seemed especially troubling in the early going. Every Auburn fan has seen our team lose to Georgia in a game when we did not think we possibly could. In previous years, we have heard our players say they cared more about beating Georgia than Alabama, but, in 2010, we had reason to think our team might be caught looking ahead, as Alabama had lost only twice, and Georgia came to Jordan-Hare Stadium with an unimpressive 5-5 record. Fortunately, true to form, our offense heated up soon enough and our team earned our first victory over Georgia since 2005. Ending Georgia's four-year streak against us was not the only significance of the win. Auburn walked off the field that day the SEC Western Division Champions for the first time since 2004. We were headed to Atlanta, and we also knew we were one win away from making the SEC

Championship Game a BCS Championship semi-final.[10] When the clock read all zeroes on Nov. 13, we entered into an almost two week waiting period before facing Alabama.

Our previous two matchups with the Tied provided two very different flavors of extreme disappointment. In 2008, we looked like we did not belong on the same field with them, or, at least that is how it looked in the second half. Oddly enough, only a well-timed piece of chicanery by the bammer coach at the end of the first half kept us from getting on the board and capturing a small piece of locker room momentum. By the end of the day, however, bama was beating us with even their backup quarterback. Seven years of prosperity evaporated in an instant; the Streak moved from present to past; only Tim Tebow and Urban Meyer stood between the bammers and a shot at a BCS Championship.

The 2009 game was an entirely different situation. We led by 14-0 fairly early, and 21-7 slightly later; obviously, we were in position to win the game. The big plays featuring Terrell Zachery, Chris Todd, and Darvin Adams elicited from Auburn fans a level of excited response few of us would have expected to experience that day. The second half, again, was our undoing. That loss was so difficult to stomach in part because we knew we had been just one play away from winning. By one play I do not mean merely the attempted Hail Mary, or even Alabama's go-ahead touchdown. Rather, we just needed one more play somewhere in the second half, whether one more first down, or one more third down stop, or perhaps something on special teams. We played a team that was freight training toward a BCS Championship, and we came up short by only one play. Our pride was much more intact after the 2009 loss than after 2008, but, the consequences were greater. We had an opportunity to derail

---

[10] At least with regards to us.

55

bama's trip to a perfect season, and, this time, Florida failed to pick up our slack. But, in 2010, we were the ones preparing to visit our rival with an undefeated record and a chance to play for a BCS Championship on the line.

What psalms find their place in those 12 days between beating Georgia and playing Alabama? Because we were preparing to face our enemy, the psalms of imprecation will be read as we look back upon that interlude. *Imprecation* is a term generally defined as "curse" or "the act of speaking a curse." In the psalms, the requests by the psalmists that God enact vengeance upon the psalmists' enemies so as to deliver the community from oppression or distress and to correct injustice are called imprecatory psalms or psalms of imprecation. These psalms make some readers uncomfortable. They are often neglected in the life of the church, and are even omitted altogether from some lectionary reading collections. Various theories have been proposed regarding the proper place of the psalms of imprecation in the contemporary church. Some have argued that these psalms still have a legitimate function in the church today so long as some certain mindset determines how we read them. In effect, we will take a similar approach in this book, as we will read the psalms of imprecation as an Auburn fan with a very specific caveat in mind.

The prayers of the speaker in the psalms of imprecation are sometimes graphic (e.g. Ps 137:8-9, "O Daughter of Babylon, doomed to destruction, happy is he who repays you for what you have done to us— he who seizes your infants and dashes them against the rocks"; Ps 58:10, "The righteous will be glad when they are avenged, when they bathe their feet in the blood of the wicked"). In our reading the psalms of imprecation as Auburn fans, we will not read the speakers' prayers for the destruction of the enemies and the wicked as prayers for the destruction of our personal enemy (bammers), but rather as petitions to God to destroy the ideology harbored and promulgated by bammers, that being the "rightful place," entitlement mindset. We are right to pray for the defeat and even eradication of this mindset, for it is beneficial to no one, and detrimental to all. Whenever someone believes that they deserve to be rewarded and to attain good things in life for no good reason (contra the Creed), they are not motivated to set high goals or work toward them on their own initiative. Those who buy into "rightful place" do not achieve their potential in life because they believe that they are entitled to luxuries, privileges, and accolades of all types, as well as overt respect not on account of their own efforts and successes, but due to the work of others (such as Paul Bryant, Gene Stallings, Mike Shula, or whomever) or simply for no reason at all. Unfortunately, every time Alabama wins a football game, this mindset is further validated in the minds of those who either just do not know any better, have been brainwashed to that end, who have adopted the entitlement philosophy after losing hope that they will achieve success on their own behalf, or simply have decided that they are not willing to make the sacrifices that lead to excellence.[11] The entitlement philosophy raises one up in his own eyes, but it holds a man or woman back in what he or she will actually accomplish and in what he or she will contribute to society. Accordingly, we need not edit the psalms of imprecation and their violent language if we are praying them against such a philosophy, praying that this philosophy will be proven false so that it will be abandoned by those who suffer on account of ascribing to it. Perhaps one day the University of Alabama at Tuscaloosa, and particularly its football program, will cease to promote this mindset. If that day ever comes, then the distinction between Auburn and Alabama will no longer be as it is described in this work, and the accompanying aspect of seeing bammers as

---

[11] see Pat Dye and John Logue, *In the Arena* (Montgomery: Black Belt Press, 1992).

the enemies of the psalmists will be obsolete. Such a changed reality is something for which we should all hope and pray. The extent of UAT's influence is such that, were they to no longer promulgate the entitlement mindset, in time, such a significant portion of the state's populace would be liberated from that way of thinking that the contributions to the greater good by the state as a whole would increase dramatically. Unfortunately, with only history and the present as the perspectives from which we can evaluate the situation, bammers do in fact liken themselves to the enemies of the psalmist, and our reading of the psalms of imprecation will conceive of those whom the speakers wish to see destroyed to be the "rightful place," entitlement mindset.

Psalm 35

Of David.

[1] Contend, O LORD, with those who contend with me;
 fight against those who fight against me.
[2] Take up shield and buckler;
 arise and come to my aid.
[3] Brandish spear and javelin
 against those who pursue me.
Say to my soul,
 "I am your salvation."

[4] May those who seek my life
 be disgraced and put to shame;
may those who plot my ruin
 be turned back in dismay.
[5] May they be like chaff before the wind,
 with the angel of the LORD driving them away;
[6] may their path be dark and slippery,
 with the angel of the LORD pursuing them.
[7] Since they hid their net for me without cause

and without cause dug a pit for me,
8 may ruin overtake them by surprise—
may the net they hid entangle them,
may they fall into the pit, to their ruin.
9 Then my soul will rejoice in the LORD
and delight in his salvation.
10 My whole being will exclaim,
"Who is like you, O LORD?
You rescue the poor from those too strong for them,
the poor and needy from those who rob them."

11 Ruthless witnesses come forward;
they question me on things I know nothing about.
12 They repay me evil for good
and leave my soul forlorn.
13 Yet when they were ill, I put on sackcloth
and humbled myself with fasting.
When my prayers returned to me unanswered,
14 I went about mourning
as though for my friend or brother.
I bowed my head in grief
as though weeping for my mother.
15 But when I stumbled, they gathered in glee;
attackers gathered against me when I was unaware.
They slandered me without ceasing.
16 Like the ungodly they maliciously mocked;
they gnashed their teeth at me.
17 O Lord, how long will you look on?
Rescue my life from their ravages,
my precious life from these lions.
18 I will give you thanks in the great assembly;
among throngs of people I will praise you.

19 Let not those gloat over me
who are my enemies without cause;
let not those who hate me without reason

maliciously wink the eye.
20 They do not speak peaceably,
   but devise false accusations
   against those who live quietly in the land.
21 They gape at me and say, "Aha! Aha!
   With our own eyes we have seen it."

22 O LORD, you have seen this; be not silent.
   Do not be far from me, O Lord.
23 Awake, and rise to my defense!
   Contend for me, my God and Lord.
24 Vindicate me in your righteousness, O LORD my God;
   do not let them gloat over me.
25 Do not let them think, "Aha, just what we wanted!"
   or say, "We have swallowed him up."

26 May all who gloat over my distress
   be put to shame and confusion;
   may all who exalt themselves over me
   be clothed with shame and disgrace.
27 May those who delight in my vindication
   shout for joy and gladness;
   may they always say, "The LORD be exalted,
   who delights in the well-being of his servant."
28 My tongue will speak of your righteousness
   and of your praises all day long.

(vv. 1-3) Using imperatives, the psalmist recruits the Lord to his fight, to take up weapons against the psalmist's enemies. As the psalmists has spoken in other psalms to his soul, here he asks the Lord to speak to his soul words of ultimate assurance, "I am your salvation." Going into the Alabama game, despite the incredible performances of our players and coaches throughout the season, we would have been foolish to place our hope in men; we needed the Lord to join in the battle, to contend with our enemy.

(vv. 4-6) The psalmist speaks a curse against those who wish him dead. The language is strongest is vv. 5 and 6, wishing the enemies to be the hunted prey of the angel of the Lord. This type of language, of course, we do not use against our enemies themselves, but we acknowledge that the harmful ideology they promote cannot be made "like chaff before the wind" by our efforts; only divine intervention can bring this about.

(vv. 7-8) The psalmist calls for a *lex talionis* type of justice, praying that the enemies' own acts of treachery be their undoing. We can pray the same against the "rightful place" ideology, hoping that it be relegated to what is indeed its "rightful place" – the place of abandoned fallacies.

(vv. 9-10) Here the psalmist turns his words to praise of the Lord, declaring it to be part of his character to intervene on behalf of those under assault. Like the psalmist, the Auburn fan, too, can "rejoice in the Lord and delight in his salvation," knowing that ultimately good will triumph over evil.

(vv. 11-16) The speaker lays out the direct contrast between his behavior toward the enemies and the enemies behavior towards the psalmist. If we are reading the enemies in this psalm to be the "rightful place" ideology, we cannot claim that "when they were ill, I put on sackcloth and humbled myself with fasting." This is simply part of the distinction between the psalmist's words, directed at actual persons, and our reading of this psalm as Auburn fans, praying the same words against an ideology espoused by persons. For these verses, we can only admire the selflessness of the speaker, and aspire to such model behavior with regards to our enemies themselves.

(vv. 17-18) In v. 17 the psalmist refocuses on the Lord, again asking *how long*. The psalmist knows that nothing escapes the notice of the Lord. He knows that God sees the malice of the wicked and wonders how long until God will intervene. In v. 18 the speaker declares confidently in advance that God will deliver him, and accordingly looks forward to publicly giving thanks.

(vv. 19-21) These verses are one of many instances in the Psalms where the verboseness of the enemies is emphasized. They gloat, speak maliciously, and falsely accuse. This type of behavior is very much a part of who the enemies are in the Psalms. Behavior such as this is also often exhibited by bammers, usually in connection with the "rightful place," entitlement philosophy. Verses 19-21 are in effect a request by the psalmist that God silence the hateful speech of the enemies. Bammers are never silent for very long, but, beating them does, in some cases, at least dampen their rhetoric temporarily, and so we are right to pray for victory over them, so as to slow the proliferation of their harmful ideology.

(vv. 22-25) This section reiterates the characterization of the enemies in vv. 19-21 in combination with a prayer for God to intervene and to vindicate the psalmist. In v. 25 the speaker imagines the enemies as desiring to say "Aha, just what we wanted." It is very easy to imagine words along these lines in the mouth of a bammer regarding UAT's opportunity to blemish our perfect season.

(vv. 26-28) The speaker distinguishes between those who celebrate his distress and those who shout for joy in responses to the psalmist's vindication. In v. 27 it is made clear that all the honor and glory pertaining to such vindication is due not to the psalmist nor the community, but to the Lord. We would be wise to take this same attitude with regards to our vindication – it is not to our credit, but should result in praise to God.

The psalms of imprecation, like the psalms of lament, acknowledge that the only viable help for the psalmists against his or her enemies is from God. The psalms of imprecation are distinguished from laments in that they emphasize specific requests to God that he intervene in such as way as to provide for the deliverance of the psalmist or the community by defeating the enemies. With regards to our 2010 team, we had plenty of reasons to be confident. Our record against the Tied in games played at Tuscaloosa provided additional temptation to think that we could, by our own strength and devices, bring about our own deliverance and vindication. But let any self-confidence be confronted by the words of Ps 94:17, "Unless the LORD had given me help, I would soon have dwelt in the silence of death." We would have been naïve to not think that our enemies had hid a net for us and dug a pit in preparation to trap us. In approaching the Alabama game, we acknowledge the need for God's help, and we ask him to contend with those who contend with us, in hopes that, by beating our enemies, we will slow the proliferation of the entitlement mindset that harms those who ascribe to it. Because our imprecation is not against the bammmers themselves, but rather against their ideology, particularly as it differs from the Creed, we do not hesitate to embrace the violent language of psalms of imprecation; we do not shy away from asking God to "Brandish spear and javelin against those who pursue me."

8

THOSE WHO CONTEND WITH US

On November 26, 2010, thousands of Auburn fans took to the highways for a trip to a place we generally try to avoid. I do not like Tuscaloosa. I do not like even zipping past it on the interstate on my way to points further west. Of course, why would I like Tuscaloosa? It is the locus of the "rightful place" ideology, the point of its origination from which it is promoted to, or, in the case of the intellectually and emotionally weaker, forced upon the people of the Great State of Alabama. I am thankful, however, that because UAT moved their home game site from Birmingham to Tuscaloosa, the targeted outdoor advertising along the roads to Tuscaloosa are there instead of around Birmingham, where their presence above the Magic City's sea of "script A" decals would elevate Birmingham's eyesore status beyond what anyone should be expected to endure. That being said, should we desire to feel any sympathy for bammers, reason to do so can be found simply in the fact that their home games are played in Tuscaloosa. The difference between Auburn and Tuscaloosa, and particularly between the relationships of those cities to the institutions that call them home, is strongly palpable. The City of Auburn, even in light of its exponential swelling over the last few decades, exists alongside, but distinct from, the Auburn University campus. The closeness of the city to the campus is nothing unfortunate, for downtown Auburn is as pleasant as the campus itself. By contrast, when one visits UAT, he or she gets the feeling that its campus is a part of the city of Tuscaloosa. Bammers traditionally recognized the undesirability of Tuscaloosa by playing the majority of their home games at Legion Field. Only in response to the continued decline of west Birmingham and from desire to create something of the home game atmosphere already in place in Auburn did bammers choose to forfeit one of their precious traditions and move their home games onto their own campus. Or, one could argue that at least the move of Alabama's home game against Auburn from Birmingham to Tuscaloosa was an act of tradition preservation, for likely bammers count not just playing, but beating Auburn in Birmingham among their traditions. Given Alabama's record in their home games against Auburn since 2000, had those games been played in Birmingham, said perceived tradition would, of course, be considerably damaged at this point. One might argue that bammers, in effort not to lose their perceived tradition of beating Auburn in Birmingham, replaced it with the new tradition of losing to Auburn in Tuscaloosa.

For the Auburn fans who traveled to Tuscaloosa on this last Friday of November, the history of the rivalry rode with them in their vehicles; for those who watched the game at home, it was set out on their tables among Thanksgiving leftovers; for more distant, but equally loyal fans, who listened to or monitored the game as best they could by various other means, this history flowed through the same cables or waves that transmitted the play-by-play. Still, in one way, this game was a break from history. It was the first time Auburn faced Alabama with a clear chance at ultimately playing for a BCS

Championship. Only two opponents stood between us and that opportunity. One, we would soon learn, would be playing in hopes of winning their first SEC Championship. The other, however, would be playing not to win anything, but only in hopes of beating us, for they feared nothing more than our taking their "rightful place," for they hate us without reason, for they are our enemies.

November 26 was a cold, overcast day. Providentially, I had not made the trip to Tuscaloosa in 2008, and found that some logistical changes had been made since 2006 – in short, we had to park farther away, lengthening the walk of faith that all football fans have made at some point, that is, the walk to the stadium without tickets. As we walked those miles, looking for tickets, I felt a similarity in the atmosphere to 2004 – the bammers were not expecting to win. Quickly, it was clear they had so little optimism regarding the game, that their attention was already focused solely on another matter altogether. To be fair, our attention was also divided – we were focused on finding a way into the stadium. With regards to buying tickets on the street, I have learned that the science boils down to one critical acuity, that being the ability to correctly choose between pulling the trigger early and playing the waiting game. On this particular game day, showing more confidence in my Old Man's *modus operandi* than he himself was, I pushed hard for the latter in the face of temptation to spend an exorbitant amount of money in order to get into the stadium with time to spare. As Providence would have it, as kickoff approached, we encountered a "gentleman" still holding a handful of tickets, and clearly starting to get nervous. We gave him a little more than half the amount of cash with which we had almost parted just a block earlier, and made out way to the gate. Soon, we were climbing stairs that seemed to part a crimson sea of bammers to either side. It was a feeling I knew well.

READING THE PSALMS AS AN AUBURN FAN

In 2006, a friend of mine and I bought student guest tickets. That is the only time I have witnessed someone take a little physical abuse in connection with the rivalry. Of course, it was immediately after the game and we were both holding five fingers in the air, so we were asking for it. Fortunately, my friend was able to keep his footing despite a good shove from behind which could have sent him falling onto the emptied bleachers below, and thus the only consequence is that he has the story to tell.

On this day, November 26, 2010, we got to our seats just in time to sing our fight song as the band played, letting the bammers of that section know it was going to be one of those games – they would get to experience the new tradition of losing to Auburn in Tuscaloosa with War Eagle ringing in their ears. The game began with Alabama receiving the opening kickoff. They immediately started an impressive drive, moving the ball efficiently, and soon they led 7-0. Of course, trailing early was no reason for concern; it almost seemed to be our team's preference throughout the 2010 season. I had expected that this game would be no different, and that, in fact, it might look worse in the beginning than had any other game. This was partly in response to the obvious: the Alabama players should be keyed up for the game – they knew what it was like playing with a bull's-eye on their chest as an undefeated team, and now they had the opportunity to take up the rifle. Furthermore, despite the history that established the new tradition, players believe in the home field advantage, and I expected the Tied to come out playing with confidence. I told my Dad just before the game began, "the first quarter could be ugly, but keep the faith." Given our familiarity with being down early, only to see our team right the ship again and again, sometimes to still ultimately win by 20 points or more, it was not the fact that Alabama had scored first that was disturbing, but rather the manner in which they scored: their running back walked in untouched. It was, indeed, ugly. He could see by the time he reached the line of scrimmage that he had six points, and then seemed to strut into the end zone, bringing to mind Ps 12: 8, "The wicked freely strut about when what is vile is honored among men." It certainly appeared from the way the game began that from its outcome the "rightful place" ideology might become even more honored among men, for if the bammers could steal from Auburn even this grand moment, i.e. the opportunity to play for a BCS Championship, after Auburn had failed to do the same to Alabama the year before, the entitlement philosophy espoused by UAT would be affirmed perhaps in a way it had never been so before.

Auburn's first possession of the game gave no reason to hope for a different outcome. Even in just a few plays, it looked as though the Alabama defense (really, their coaches) had figured out our offense in a way that no other opponent had been able to do. One of the CBS commentators took advantage of the first opportunity to cater to the bammers, summarizing our first possession by saying, "three and out for the vaunted Auburn offense."[12] We gave the ball back to Alabama, and it was clear that their offense had not missed a beat while on the sideline for four downs. One of the commentators then took the opportunity to say, "Auburn had a very manageable schedule until this game." Down only seven points, one bammer was already painting the picture that Alabama was exposing our entire season as illusory. Soon thereafter, Alabama's star receiver made a catch in the open field on his way to the end zone. Indeed, things were looking ugly. The opening events of the game gave us reason to call out to God in the same manner as the psalmist in Ps 25:1-2, "To you, O LORD, I lift up my soul; in you I trust, O my God. Do not let me be put to shame, nor let my enemies triumph over me." It was already clear this was a battle we

---

[12] I later watched a recording of the CBS broadcast.

could not win by means of our own strength or devices, necessitating that we look to the only one capable of establishing victory with words like those of Ps 22:19, "But you, O LORD, be not far off; O my Strength, come quickly to help me." On our next possession, it appeared as though, to that point, our prayer was not being answered. Our quarterback, the best runner in the nation, was stopped for a loss; the Alabama defender then stood up and repeatedly beat his chest with great vigor of self-adoration. Like the psalmist in Ps 10:5, we were troubled by what we saw: "His ways are always prosperous; he is haughty and your laws are far from him; he sneers at all his enemies." The bammers, of course, were jubilant. They had not come into this game expecting to win, but now they were allowing themselves to aspire to a great victory. A CBS commentator exclaimed, "I've never heard it this loud."

Shortly thereafter, it looked as though we might stop the bleeding. On third and eight, the Alabama quarterback retreated from a blitz, only to be caught and taken to the ground by the best defensive player in the country. Our defender leapt to his feet with enthusiasm, and was embraced almost immediately by a teammate, thus restricting him from inappropriately making a display for individual accolade. Nonetheless, the officials called an unsportsmanlike behavior penalty, negating the effectiveness of the play. Even a CBS commentator felt compelled to acknowledge that the particular Auburn player in question had been "targeted" in response to the complaints of those who had been unable to overcome his prowess. Given this targeting, said player might have experienced feelings like those expressed in Ps 59:3-4, "See how they lie in wait for me! Fierce men conspire against me for no offense or sin of mine, O LORD. I have done no wrong, yet they are ready to attack me. Arise to help me; look on my plight!" As the injustice of the penalty was being administered, the Alabama quarterback began applauding. He looked to be celebrating the yardage awarded as if he, or at least his team, had accomplished the gain on their own behalf. In this way he was exhibiting the "rightful place" ideology: *When our opponents earn something desirable, and we benefit from that desirable thing not being credited to them, we are deserving of that benefit, and we celebrate as if we ourselves had earned it.* Alabama went on to convert a fourth-down play, and later to score another touchdown. The Alabama quarterback threw a long fade pass that floated to his receiver in the end zone. The way the ball fell out of the sky caused one to wonder if injustice was actually descending from above. Like the speaker in Ps 37:35, we felt as though we were seeing "a wicked and ruthless man flourishing like a green tree in its native soil." How could we possibly respond to this? We were helpless to do anything but speak the words of Ps 30:10: "Hear, O LORD, and be merciful to me; O LORD, be my help."

Despite our prayers, or so it seemed, our next possession was another three and out. After third down, our quarterback, the best player in the country, who looked as though someone had managed to soak his uniform in liquid Kryptonite, hurried back to the sideline. In the arena of bammers, surely he felt what the psalmist expressed in Ps 25:19: "See how my enemies have increased and how fiercely they hate me!"

At the end of the first quarter, my Dad asked me if when I had told him the first quarter could be ugly I had anticipated it being this bad. I told him I had not. It was not the score itself that surprised me, but the way it came about. Had I not seen the first 15 minutes, and someone told me the score, I would have guessed a sequence of events along these lines: Alabama scored once on a big offensive play (as they did in actuality to go up 14-0); another score might have come after a turnover on Auburn's side of the field; the third score would be the result of a fumble after a long Auburn drive, followed by a long Alabama drive. The ugliness of the first quarter which I had not at all anticipated was this: we had yet to make a single stop against the Alabama offense and our offense had yet to make a first down. We were being dominated.

But, when hope appeared lost, when Alabama looked to surely be on their way to a 28-point lead, something happened. It was a play that at first appeared in place with all the preceding events of the game. The Alabama quarterback completed a short pass to the running back, who then found plenty of space in which to advance the ball. He moved from the middle of the field to the sideline, and looked to have a chance at a touchdown. At the very least, it looked as though the play would result in Alabama achieving a field position from which they would likely score their fourth touchdown of the day, extending their lead to 28-0. But, something happened on the way to the end zone. An Auburn player, who in a sense had already been beaten on the play, pursued the runner from behind. It was a situation in which most defensive lineman would have given up on the play, and simply watched to see what luck the secondary had preventing a big play from becoming a score. Instead, this particular defender ran after the ball carrier as though he were running for his life. Adding skill equal in extremity to his desperation, he then made a careful, deliberate, forceful strike, punching the ball out of the running back's grasp, and sending it into the path of destiny. As remarkable as the effort of that Tiger was, it was then matched by the incredulity caused by what happened next.

Now, just for the sake of engaging what happened thoroughly, or possibly for the benefit of less experienced readers, allow me to break down just what occurred. A football, unlike the balls used for virtually every other sport played in America, is not spherical. When a soccer ball or a basketball or even a baseball (so long as it is beyond the infield) hits the ground, one can with a high degree of confidence predict the direction and manner in which the ball will then bounce or roll based on careful observation of the path and velocity of the ball prior to hitting the ground. This is not true with a football. A football is oblong. Its circumference is widest at the middle and then tapers in each direction all the way down to a point. It is as if the ball were designed for unpredictability. This is why the expression "which way the ball bounces" is used to describe the determination of a hotly contested football game and not for close games of other sports. There are times when one does not know whether a football is going to bounce left, right, forward or backwards at any potential degree in between, straight up, or just stop. The Auburn defender punched the ball out at about the 20 yard line. It flew through the air, and then hit the ground just inside the 10 yard line. The ball then bounced and rolled within a few feet of the sideline straight ahead into the end zone. Had the ball gone out-of-bounds anywhere between the 20 yard line and the goal line, possession would have been retained by the last team to have established possession, which in this case would have been the offense, i.e. Alabama. The ball not only made it into the end zone, but continued in a generally straight-ahead direction; two Auburn players were attempting to corral the ball as it went out the back of the end zone. The 10 yards the ball travelled in the end zone were not needed from the Auburn fan's point of view. In fact, had the ball entered the end zone, and then bounced to the right, out of bounds, Auburn still would have taken over possession. The distance traveled by the ball in the end zone only provided opportunity for Alabama to recover the ball there, which would have resulted in an Alabama touchdown. Because Alabama did not recover, the final 10 yards the ball traveled serve to emphasize the improbability of the event. As Auburn fans, we had to wonder if God had answered the prayer of Ps 86:17: "Give me a sign of your goodness, that my enemies may see it and be put to shame, for you, O LORD, have helped me and comforted me." A CBS commentator pointed out that it was the right hand of the Auburn defender who punched out the ball, but the commentators did not discuss the improbable path the ball took after being punched out, for, if they had, it might have constituted allusion to another right hand at work; cf. Ps 20:6: "Now I know that the LORD saves his anointed; he answers him from his holy heaven with the saving power of his right hand."

As Auburn's offense came back onto the field, a CBS commentator, rather than emphasizing the opportunity provided by the great defensive play, declared that to this point in the game "their offense has done *nada*." CBS then showed footage of one play from the Georgia game and explained how it illustrated a flaw in our quarterback's mechanics. It was as if CBS were attempting to reassure bammers that, despite what had just happened, UAT was still the better team, and was still in control. But, then something else happened. It was not as remarkable as a punched ball traveling straight forward for 20 yards after hitting the ground; in fact, it was undoubtedly unnoticed for what it was by many fans on both sides – we made our first first down of the game. The significance here cannot be overstated – we had just made our first stop of the game, and we followed that by converting our first first down. If the bleeding had not been stopped, perhaps it had at least been slowed. Could this be a sign that a differently looking second half was soon to come? We hoped it was a sign that God was answering the prayer of Ps 38:21-22: "O LORD, do not forsake me; be not far from me, O my God. Come quickly to help me, O Lord my Savior."

Alabama got the ball back and again started moving down the field. Their quarterback improved to 12 for 12 passing on the day. It again appeared that Alabama was surely about to take a 28-point lead. Watching in dread, the emotions Auburn fans were experiencing are well expressed by Ps 69:3, "I am worn out calling for help; my throat is parched. My eyes fail, looking for my God." In that moment, when it seemed like God was not interested in our battle against "rightful place" ideology, we had to wonder whether the earlier incident of apparent divine intervention should be attributed, as it has by many, simply to the earthly laws of chance. It had only been a temporary reprieve for our suffering, a delay of the inevitable.

But, then something else happened. The Alabama quarterback took the snap, dropped back a few steps, and threw the ball to his left, where an Alabama running back was waiting for it right on the goal line with no defender near enough to affect the play in any way. In the second or so it took the ball to travel from the quarterback's hand to the goal line, it looked certain that our enemies had taken a 4-touchdown lead. We had seen our team overtake leading opponents in most of our games throughout the season, but 4 touchdowns just seemed like too much. Instead of a comeback, a 4-touchdown lead seems more likely to lead to fifth, sixth, and seventh touchdowns. This was a frightening prospect. As Providence would have it, however, the Alabama running back must have found it frightening as well, for the ball hit his hands, but then fell to the earth. After failing to score on second or third down, the bammers settled for a field goal. Once again, we had to wonder why we had yet to be exterminated by our enemies when they looked to be so clearly on the precipice of crushing all hope. The words of Ps 94:18-19 come to mind: "When I said, 'My foot is slipping,' your love, O LORD, supported me. When anxiety was great within me, your consolation brought joy to my soul."

The Auburn offense took to the field again, this time trailing 24-0. Their preceding possession had been more productive than any previous, even by only resulting in one first down. On this possession, on a third-and-five play, an Auburn receiver, a player who had borne the burden of

2008's misery in a distinct way, made an impressive catch to keep the drive going. Still, the Alabama defense continued to play well against our running game. One of our running backs took a lick that elicited excited moans from the bammer crowd; a CBS commentator described it by saying our player got "popped"; the bammers might have thought it would prove to be the hit of the day. Our quarterback, too, continued to find advancing the ball on the ground to be difficult, but was able to rely on his arm. The same receiver who made the grab on third and five hauled in another impressive catch. A few plays after a CBS commentator exclaimed that our quarterback "can't get loose today," another Auburn receiver got loose down the sideline. With 5:08 remaining in the first half, the game was forever changed. Auburn was on the scoreboard. In Ps 5:1-3, the psalmist implores, "Give ear to my words, O LORD, consider my sighing. Listen to my cry for help, my King and my God, for to you I pray. In the morning, O LORD, you hear my voice; in the morning I lay my requests before you and wait in expectation." Could it be that the Lord had indeed heard our cry for help? Finally seeing our offense generate a few points gave us the smallest particle of hope that the game to that point appeared to soundly deny.

Immediately thereafter, however, it looked as though we might have been given hope in vain, as Alabama responded by again moving the ball effectively, all the way to inside our 10-yard line. Here I feel there is something I must confess. There was a moment as I stood in the stands of that stadium on the campus of UAT, and I do not remember at what point in the game it was, though it would make sense for it to be at this moment, for it appeared that Alabama was about to answer our first score by securing a 31-7 lead, when I doubted not just the existence of the God of the Bible, but of any God or god at all. What I was witnessing just seemed too unjust for any divine being to oversee. Given the strong sense of theism in my psyche, I quickly moved from doubting the existence of God to somber acceptance that He must be an Alabama fan. I could think of no other explanation. But, if God were proving himself a supporter of the Tied, it certainly was not producing any enthusiasm among the bammers in the stadium. While it looked like their team was about to put the game potentially out of reach, the bammers were as quiet as they had been at any moment in the game to this point; there was nothing to be excited about – they had already won. We had hoped their mouths would be shut (cf. Ps 31:18, "Let their lying lips be silenced, for with pride and contempt they speak arrogantly against the righteous"), but this is not what we had in mind. But not all the bammers were resting for the post-game celebration: CBS returned from a commercial break to a shot of the Alabama quarterback's family dancing in the bleachers. On the next play, the best defensive player in the country caused the Alabama QB to fumble. In yet another bizarre moment, the ball rested on the ground undisturbed at the heels of an unknowing Alabama player for a period of about 1.5 seconds which seemed to take about 5 minutes to pass. Our defender then army crawled from where he had landed after causing the fumble to retake possession for our team. The involvement of a higher power once again appeared evident. How were we to respond? Though obviously too soon to get too excited, the sense of relief was very real, prompting a sense of gratitude like that found in Ps 28:6-7: "Praise be to the LORD, for he has heard my cry for mercy. The LORD is my strength and my shield; my heart trusts in him, and I am helped. My heart leaps for joy and I will give thanks to him in song."

The Auburn offense took the field for one more possession in the half. Instead of voluntarily limping into the locker room, we tried to make something happen, which only resulted in our quarterback being sacked. Now, the bammers made some noise as they prepared to spend halftime already celebrating a victory.[13] With regards to the rivalry, they had successfully defended their BCS Championship. They were still in their "rightful place."

The second half started in much the same fashion as the first half ended: our quarterback again being dropped for a loss. The bammers gleefully rejoiced. The halftime victory celebration continued. On the next play, the celebration was over. Our quarterback again showed that running was not his only skill. Yet another receiver was on the end of this pass, and his determination to make it to the end zone would not be denied. In a game that just moments ago had been on the brink of 31-7, the two teams were now separated by only 10 points. Though they would hope against hope the remainder of the afternoon, from my observation of the bammers surrounding me, it was at this point they realized their team was going the way of our previous 11 opponents. Delusional as they are, even bammers had seen throughout the 2010 season that to be within striking distance of this Auburn team was to be outside the realm of possible escape, to even be in the crosshairs already meant certain death. Conversely, though conventional wisdom urged us to restrain our optimism, we also knew it was already time for the words of Ps 86:12-13: "I will praise you, O Lord my God, with all my heart; I will glorify your name forever. For great is your love toward me; you have delivered me from the depths of the grave."

For the next few possessions, the game resembled a traditional Iron Bowl, meaning the teams exchanged punts. But soon Auburn would act out of turn. After an impressive drive, our quarterback carried the ball into the end zone. After he crossed the goal line, a small flourish of monopoly money erupted from the bleachers beyond the back of the

---

[13] See Vasha Hunt's photo on p. 88 of *Boda Getta: Auburn's Remarkable Run*, produced by the Opelika-Auburn News.

end zone. This action was curious for at least a couple of reasons. Firstly, it was, of course, planned ahead of time: an agreement made between some number of bammers to attempt to convey some ill-spirited connotation in a visible way. Furthermore, it was clear that this moment had been the one in mind all along – the first rushing touchdown by our quarterback. The begged question here is obvious: since when do bammers assume that the other team will score at all, let alone that a particular player will score in a particular way? Also, one has to imagine they expected this score to occur earlier in the game, when their display could have, ideally from a bammer perspective, constituted some type of psychological assault along the lines of *you may have scored, but we know your scoring to be illegitimate*. Having had to wait until the third quarter to activate their plan, it seems they would have been wiser to abandon it altogether, for what use could such a ploy be against a player who had just narrowed a 24-point gap down to only 3? They may as well have been throwing confetti for our championship parade. Secondly, I said above that the atmosphere before the game indicated that the bammers did not expect to win. For anyone who might have found this implausible, and that is understandable given the bammers' usually unrelenting overconfidence, he or she must acknowledge that at least this small sampling of bammers expected to lose the game, for why else would they have sought to publicize their excuse for losing?

For those whose prayers had only an hour or so ago sounded like Ps 144:11, "Deliver me and rescue me from the hands of foreigners whose mouths are full of lies, whose right hands are deceitful," our words turned more and more to praise, such as those of Ps 96:10-12, "Let those who love the LORD hate evil, for he guards the lives of his faithful ones and delivers them from the hand of the wicked. Light is shed upon the righteous and joy on the upright in heart. Rejoice in the LORD, you who are righteous, and praise his holy name" and Ps 107:5-6, "They were hungry and thirsty, and their lives ebbed away. Then they cried out to the LORD in their trouble, and he delivered them from their distress."

On the bammers' next possession, their offense looked like ours had in the 1st quarter. Whereas in the early stages of the game the bammers reigned down their chorus of *whoooo* in response to catches made by their star wide receiver, now they would have more appropriately responded with *wherrrr*, as in *where is our offense?* Our defense stood them up, forcing Alabama to punt, but the punt was muffed, and Alabama recovered the ball on our side of the field. The CBS commentator excitedly exclaimed "Oh, man!" The bammers had gotten their break – maybe this would be their day after all. In that moment, they envisioned a return to their "rightful place." In addition to one opportunity to go up 31-7, the bammers now had their third chance of the day to reach or exceed 28 points, but that chance slipped away, and they kicked a field goal. Our words continued to be filled increasingly with praise. Consider Ps 116:8-9: "For you, O LORD, have delivered my soul from death, my eyes from tears, my feet from stumbling, that I may walk before the LORD in the land of the living."

After the field goal, the score was 27-21 with Alabama, as they had been since very early in the game, still in the lead. On the ensuing possession, the Auburn offense began moving the ball, and the drive was still in progress as the third quarter reached its conclusion. As is their tradition, the bammers all held up 4 fingers, so as to declare that the fourth quarter would belong to them, and that on this day they would finish the job in the fourth quarter and deny Auburn the opportunity of moving the BCS Champions' throne from Tuscaloosa to the "loveliest village of the plain." As they held up 4 fingers, little did they know that if they only could have held on to what had earlier been a 24-point lead, they would have avoided finishing the season 4th in the SEC Western

Division. As it would come to pass, in one year, the bammers would fall from 1st in the BCS to 4th in the West.

Continuing this numeric theme, Auburn soon faced a fourth down decision. With 13:49 left to play in the game, Auburn had 4th and 3 at the Alabama 47-yard line. All things considered, conventional football wisdom would have called for a punt. Since the 2nd quarter, when Alabama failed on their second opportunity to reach 28 points, the tenor of the game had changed such that Alabama had moved from scoring touchdowns to kicking field goals (at best), and Auburn had moved from punting to scoring touchdowns and playing well on defense. With the bulk of the 4th quarter still to be played and an opportunity to surrender possession but only by giving our opponent the ball (ideally) somewhere inside their own 20-yard line, it would make sense to punt here, and to show patience in waiting for the right moment to take the lead. In this decision we see the intangible nature of coaching. It is not always about following the prescribed rules of strategy. Sometimes the crux of the matter is to recognize the heightened significance of a critical point in the game. These points appear to all but the most astute to be like any other down, or, even if they are seen to be a moment of great significance, they are still not appreciated for the full value which most of us can only assign to them in retrospect. Coach Chizik and Coach Malzahn recognized the critical nature of this moment in the game with an acumen that, in all fairness, among the remaining 100,000+ people at the stadium, was likely shared by only Coach Saban. We are all familiar with the idiom "playing to win instead of playing not to lose." In this situation, it would be correct to say that Chizik and Malzahn were coaching to take the game from the opponent instead of waiting and hoping for the opponent to give the game away.[14] Still, to reduce their decision making in this situation to even this maxim fails to properly acknowledge their clairvoyance. So many situational coaching decisions are made in the days or weeks prior to the game. My belief is that, for this decision, the choice was made on the spot, in the moment, with an uncanny perception that if we were going to win a BCS Championship, we needed to convert this 4th down. It was a gutsy call, but a smart one. We played to our strengths: we let our soon to be Heisman-winning quarterback throw a strike to a receiver in whom we had full confidence. With this play, the game really began to take on the feeling that would define it in the end. It was time for Auburn, like the speaker of Ps 108:13, to say, "With God we will gain the victory, and he will trample down our enemies." On the very next play, our quarterback, largely stymied by the Alabama defense on the ground throughout the game, ran for a gain of 13 yards. Whereas earlier events in the game had brought to mind the words of Ps 37:35, "I have seen a wicked and ruthless man flourishing like a green tree in its native soil," we now began to understand that the reality of the following verse was beginning to emerge before our eyes: "but he soon passed away and was no more; though I looked for him, he could not be found." A few plays later, with 11:55 remaining to play, our quarterback completed a pass to our tight end who had executed a block-then-release maneuver to perfection. The extra point was good, and for the first time in the game, Auburn was in the lead.

---

[14] At Sunday school, two days after the game, I was told by an educated bammer that what made him so sick about the loss was that Auburn had not won the game, but rather Alabama had utterly and totally given it away. I wish he could have gone into the Alabama locker room Friday evening and chastised the coaches and players for giving the game away. I wonder what their response would have been?

When we went ahead, it seemed extremely unlikely to me that we could win the game without scoring again. Though our defense had played well in the second half, I simply could not imagine Alabama not finding a way to answer our score, thus putting the onus back on our offense to determine the outcome of the game. The reality, of course, was that we were already experiencing the blessing described in Ps 18:37-42: "I pursued my enemies and overtook them; I did not turn back till they were destroyed. I crushed them so that they could not rise; they fell beneath my feet. You armed me with strength for battle; you made my adversaries bow at my feet. You made my enemies turn their backs in flight, and I destroyed my foes. They cried for help, but there was no one to save them— to the LORD, but he did not answer. I beat them as fine as dust borne on the wind; I poured them out like mud in the streets."

Once we took the lead, it was never surrendered. This reminds me of the last time an undefeated Auburn team played in Tuscaloosa. The comparable situation in 2004 was different not so much in kind as in degree. Though we took the lead about 15 minutes earlier in that game, and UAT had only been up by 6, the earliest moments of the 2004 game had a similar feel to 2010 in that the bammers had not expected to win, and when they were able to manage the first two scores of the game, even though each was only a field goal, they were delightfully surprised and dared to think that they had an opportunity to ruin our perfect season. In that game, once Carnell Williams crossed the goal line, and John Vaughn made the extra point, Auburn was on top, never again to trail.

And so it would be in 2010. Still, for one Alabama player, there was more than just the game remaining to be lost. As expected, the Alabama offense showed some life in their first possession of the game playing from behind. After making one first down and appearing to have converted another, the Tied was penalized for an illegal shift, bringing up a 3rd-and-six play on which an Alabama player stretched the ball forward near enough to the needed yardage to require a measurement. When the chain showed the play to have ended just short of a first down, the bammers' chorus of *whoooo* now became *booooo*, for they had not expected the officials to actually measure the gain accurately; they expected to be given a first down which would assists them in regaining their "rightful place." All the same, Alabama made a first down on 4th and inches, prompting a CBS commentator to exclaim "how about this!" in his excitement that perhaps the Tied were on their way to retaking the lead. Indeed, Alabama made yet another first down, drawing near to the Auburn 30-yard line, and it seemed we surely would need to score again to win the game.

But, one more time, something happened on the way to the end zone. This time the lights went out, at least for the Alabama quarterback. A 182-pound defensive back for Auburn came off the strong end, grabbed the Alabama quarterback by the arm and around the waist, and threw him to the ground. The quarterback did not get up. Watching the action from a distance, I at first imagined that the injured player might have had his shoulder dislocated. As the seconds turned to minutes, it became clear the injury must be of a different nature. The atmosphere in the stadium was unlike anything I had ever experienced. Both tense and reverently silent, the vibe given off collectively by my surrounding bammers reminded me of that described in interviews by those who stood in shock at Dealey Plaza after the departure of the motorcade. What we later learned was that the quarterback had suffered a concussion, which, of course, is an injury associated with cognitive difficulties, including memory loss.

Just as there were three trainers who assisted the quarterback off the field,[15] so are there three references in the Psalms to the memory of the wicked being wiped away: Ps 9:6: "Endless ruin has overtaken the enemy, you have uprooted their cities; even the memory of them has perished"; Ps 34:16: "the face of the LORD is against those who do evil, to cut off the memory of them from the earth"; and, Ps 109:5: "May their sins always remain before the LORD, that he may cut off the memory of them from the earth." Also, the moment when the lights went out symbolizes three erasures of memory regarding the rivalry. Firstly, the memory of our dismay over Alabama's 2009 BCS Championship was cleared from our minds. Because this play both ended Alabama's last scoring opportunity, and removed their starting quarterback from the game, it effectively signaled what the outcome of the game would be, and subsequently provided the assurance that Alabama would not successfully prevent Auburn from winning the very Championship which Alabama had hoped to defend. Secondly, the memory of the feeling we had in the first half that God was allowing our enemy to triumph over us was also wiped clean, as it suddenly became crystal clear that it mattered not who had led the first 48 minutes, 5 seconds of the game. Thirdly, the former name of the venue in which the game was being played, Tuberville-Denny Stadium, was also forgotten in favor of its new name, Tuberville-Chizik Stadium.[16]

---

[15] http://www.youtube.com/watch?v=RqI-xpP2OMo

[16] One might argue that the way Tuberville ended his tenure at Auburn should revoke the honoring of his name in this way. My rebuttal is that, his numerous flaws and misgivings notwithstanding, we cannot deny how fun it was to experience the Streak and to see Tuberville maintain Auburn's undefeated record in Tuscaloosa through the first four games played there in the contemporary era. Additionally, regardless of Tuberville's other disappointments, his 7-3 record against Alabama is enviable among the history of Auburn

Some consider the Alabama quarterback getting his bell rung to be just deserts for his making an obscene gesture to a section of Auburn fans. My viewing of the various bird videos along with my memory of witnessing the event cause me to judge the evidence as to whether he actually made such a gesture as inconclusive. There is no need to determine whether or not the quarterback deserved to get knocked out. It was a clean play, and every player on the field assumes the risks inherent to a collision sport. Yet, for those who want to point at some action by the Alabama quarterback to show that he had it coming, I recommend his applause earlier in the game for what he knew was a crock call or even his reaction to throwing a needless touchdown pass against us near the end of the 2008 game.

Once the quarterback was successfully escorted to the bench, the Alabama punt team came onto the field. There would be no muff this time. In fact, the Alabama punter honored his program's late-modern claim to 13 national championships with a 13-yard punt.

On our final non-kneel-down possession of the game, our quarterback was able to get a first down, keeping the clock in motion. We did eventually have to punt, giving the Tied, with their backup quarterback, a chance at what would have been an incredible finish. Instead, they threw 4 incompletions, one of which would have been an interception if not for an outstanding play by the intended receiver. Our defender on that play was the same player who had knocked

---

coaches. Accordingly, I choose to remember the good times with Tubs in this manner. One might also argue that only one win by Chizik in Tuscaloosa is not enough to earn him a place in the title of what some call Jordan-Hare West. This point is well taken, but I argue that the way in which we won that one game, combined with its significance to Auburn's first BCS Championship, justifies his being so honored.

out Alabama's starting quarterback. If he had successfully made the interception, his already indelible stamp upon the outcome and character of the game would have been elevated . . . well, actually, this is more of an infinity-plus-one contemplation: the significance of T'Sharvan Bell's impact on the game cannot be any greater than it already is any more than can that of Antoine Carter.

At the game's conclusion, the bammers stood in silence. Nobody moved. We dared not either; we knew at that point our wisest course of action was to keep as low a profile as possible. One bammer in the throes of having lost a 24-point lead along with the opportunity to keep Auburn out of their "rightful place" had already shown me his bark in a personal way, and, while I was Fairley confident there was no accompanying bite, let alone one of equal ferocity, I had no desire to put his self-restraint to the test. They stood there in shock, gazing down at the field, unsure as to whether they possessed the emotional capacity to even accept or process the reality of what they had just witnessed. The unthinkably rapturous had not been merely within their reach, but seemingly securely in their grasp. Even if they had already failed to defend their BCS Championship on a national scale, it had appeared that they would at least manage to do so within the boundaries of a single state. Alabama had never lost a game after leading by so many points. Even the oldest of those in attendance had never seen anything so horrible. The strangeness of the immediate postgame response is that it had seemed as though once the lead had been cut to 10 points that the bammers around us realized they would lose the game. To be fair, there is a difference between recognizing impending doom and actually seeing it come to pass. Perhaps it was the "rightful place" mentality that caused them to still exhibit surprise at the end of the game, for, while intellectually they may have understood they had lost before the clock read all zeroes, emotionally they persisted in expecting to be given a win, even if in the final minute with their offense being led by an inexperienced quarterback, simply because they were entitled to such a result. Their state of shock brings to mind Ps 55:9, "Confuse the wicked, O Lord, confound their speech" and Ps 107:42, "The upright see and rejoice, but all the wicked shut their mouths."[17]

The 2010 Auburn-Alabama game was unlike any in the history of the rivalry. It is difficult to imagine that any future meeting will provide the same type or level of incredulity. Looking back on the first 11 games of the 2010 season, perhaps we should not be so surprised that this team would win their final regular season game in such fashion. Having amazed us in so many ways and moments throughout the season, a 24-point comeback was the only way they could end the regular schedule with a bang – it was the only thing they could do to create a grand finale. The story of this game is one which words cannot adequately tell. Having relived it to the extent that I have over the last few days in order to write this chapter has ultimately caused me concern that at any moment I might wake up and learn that November 26, 2010 was only a dream – a vivid, wonderful, sublime fabrication grown out of the deepest, strongest desires of my subconscious.

The comeback, in a generic sense, has always been sports' greatest dramatic element. It is the one sports metaphor so pervasively applied to stories outside the sports world. Comebacks tell the stories of groups or individuals who overcome the greatest of obstacles to rise like the Phoenix from defeat and despair to the loftiest heights of human experience. They are the stories that remind us that anything is possible. By overcoming a 24-point deficit against the defending BCS Champion, the team (really, the people

---

[17] This may remind the reader of a gesture made by one of our players on the field following the game.

group) who wanted more than any other to steal from us our chance at supreme honor, who was still a top-ten ranked opponent,[18] we redefined the entire comeback genre. The twelfth win of Auburn's 2010 season is now the zenith to which all other comebacks will look upward in awe and admiration. The living history of this game will ultimately raise it to a place in the folklore of Auburn Football presently occupied by only the 1972 game. How are we to respond to something so magnificent? Coach Chizik, in his first words to Tracy Wolfson after the game, said it best: "God is good."

---

[18] At least in the AP.

Smith-Wallace Field at Tuberville-Chizik Stadium.

9

BUT, WHAT ABOUT CAM NEWTON?

Oh, yes, Cam Newton – did we pay him $180,000 or compensate him in any improper way to play football for Auburn University? I know I did not. Did anyone else? I do not know. And, guess what – neither does any bammer. They may suspect that we did, or conclude that because Cecil Newton discussed receiving compensation from another school that he must have had a similar conversation with Auburn,[19] or simply prefer to believe that we paid him, but none of these positions is the same as actually knowing that Cam Newton or his family received any type of improper benefit in exchange for agreeing to play for our team. Because the bammers do not know that Auburn or Newton did anything improper, and yet insisted upon repeatedly making accusations and assertions as if fact to that end, their words constitute malicious, slanderous, sinful speech. We discussed in ch. 4 how the psalmists designate verboseness as a primary characteristic of their enemies and the wicked. Here we will

---

[19] Which still does not necessitate that any compensation changed hands.

examine a specific way in which the psalmists relate their enemies to malicious speech, which will show that by slandering the Auburn Family on account of speculations regarding Cam Newton, bammers likened themselves unto the enemies of the psalmists in an especially direct way. In the psalms, enemies are regularly compared to aggressive, potentially dangerous animals. Examples include: lions (Ps 35:17, "O Lord, how long will you look on? Rescue my life from their ravages, my precious life from these lions"); dogs (Ps 22:20, "Deliver my life from the sword, my precious life from the power of the dogs"); and, snakes (Ps 58:3-4, "Even from birth the wicked go astray; from the womb they are wayward and speak lies. Their venom is like the venom of a snake"). Furthermore, these animals are specifically described as dangerous on account of the threat they pose by way of their mouth. Illustrations of this principle pertaining to lions include: Ps 22:13, "Roaring lions tearing their prey open their mouths wide against me"; Ps 22:21, "Rescue me from the mouth of the lions"; and, Ps 57:4, "I am in the midst of lions; I lie among ravenous beasts— men whose teeth are spears and arrows, whose tongues are sharp swords." In Ps 59:6 the speaker says of the nations, "They return at evening, snarling like dogs, and prowl about the city." Consider also Ps 140:1-3, "Rescue me, O LORD, from evil men; protect me from men of violence, who devise evil plans in their hearts and stir up war every day. They make their tongues as sharp as a serpent's; the poison of vipers is on their lips." From the moment the story broke until well after the BCS Championship Game (and for some unto no end) bammers could never never find enough words of castigation for Cam Newton and the Auburn Family to satisfy their vengeful lust. Again, let us assume for the sake of argument that some individual or group somehow provided some improper benefit to Cam Newton or to someone connected to Newton in exchange for Cam agreeing to play football at Auburn. Would the common Auburn supporter know anything about it? Of course not. And, how much more true is it that none of us would have had anything to do with it; we certainly were not participants or conspirators with any connection to such alleged misdeed. Even with this being the obvious reality, I would be very surprised to meet a single Auburn fan who could not at some point during November 2010 to January 2011 identify with the words of the psalmist in Ps 35:11, "Ruthless witnesses come forward; they question me on things I know nothing about." What was the bammers' motive in this incessant slandering? Was it because they are so concerned for fairness and the amateur spirit of collegiate athletics that they wanted to make sure any action injurious thereto be properly investigated? Right. It was psychological warfare. They knew they could not beat us on the field. They knew that, were the course of the season allowed to play out as it had through the first several weeks, that ultimately they would surrender their status as BCS Champion not to Florida, or Texas, or LSU or anyone else, but to Auburn – the cow college, the school down the road, etc.. It drove them nuts. They simply could not stomach it. They knew that their team could not prevent this, and neither could any other; so, they tried to get into our heads. They attempted to derail the Auburn Spirit on every level from the watercooler to SportsCenter. Any doubt as to this being the case need simply be referred to the music played by the staff at Tuberville-Chizik Stadium upon our team's arrival.[20] Furthermore, anyone who would criticize me for the way religion and football enthusiasm are intertwined in this book must also look at how bammers tirelessly carried their gospel of "Cam is ineligible" throughout the land with conviction and devotion of which only the Great Commission is actually worthy. For them, it truly was good news, for they knew that the possibility of Cam being ruled ineligible was the only way Auburn could either be prevented from winning the BCS

---

[20] http://www.youtube.com/watch?v=pMQ8gv8BBJA

Championship or have it revoked after the fact. This is how they encouraged (really comforted) one another as a day they had proclaimed their whole lives would never come steadily drew near. Strangely enough, their rhetoric indeed pushed into the area of proselytization, as if by persistence an Auburn fan would eventually respond, saying, "You know what, you're right. I am going to email Dr. Gogue and ask that Cam not be allowed to play, effective immediately." For bammers, at least until they were up 14-0 and thought they had a chance to win, November 26, 2010 was not so much a football game as it was a denominational convention, a mega-gathering of like-minded individuals celebrating their mantra – "Cam is ineligible!" They proudly displayed "$cam" stickers as their Tefillin. One group of bammers, apparently finding one of our players worth more of their trouble than their entire team, coordinated their body painting in celebration of the good news. This, in combination with the monopoly money mentioned in the previous chapter, plus the "$cam" stickers, and also the "$cam Newton" t-shirts being sold in Tuscaloosa while Alabama still had two opponents remaining to play before facing Auburn,[21] is representative of a community-wide effort to make an excuse for losing a game that had not yet been played, the likes of which college football may have never seen before nor will ever witness again. As I said above, I do not know for fact whether or not anyone with any connection to Auburn University provided any type of improper benefit to Cam Newton or anyone else. I do know that ESPN owes Cam at least $180,000 for the mileage they got out of the non-story during the Heisman Trophy Award Show alone. Now that the saga is behind us, perhaps we should be thinking less about who might have paid Cam Newton, and more about who Cam Newton should pay. What I mean is that, while bammers must have caused Cam to relate to the words of Ps 109:1-3, "O God, whom I praise,

---

[21] http://www.youtube.com/watch?v=5RbTH3qvsck

do not remain silent, for wicked and deceitful men have opened their mouths against me; they have spoken against me with lying tongues - With words of hatred they surround me; they attack me without cause," one could argue that Cam owes those very bammers a significant amount of money, for they certainly provided him an opportunity to display his ability to score 4 touchdowns despite the highest level of all manner of distraction, and who knows but that perhaps that display made some impact on Cam being selected as the no. 1 pick in the 2011 NFL Draft.

EXCURSUS:

THE MAN WHO WOULD HAVE BEEN QUARTERBACK

There was a time when Cam Newton was expected to take over the role of starting quarterback at Florida from Tim Tebow. While that never came to pass, Newton did take over from Tebow his role as the most talked about player in the country. Of course, not all of the conversation regarding Newton was as effusively positive as it had been concerning Tebow constantly for, really, Tebow's entire 4 years at Florida with considerable elevation over the third and fourth. In 2010, Cam Newton provided the finest ingredients to the perfect recipe for all those who wish to make college football a reality show. Firstly, he was new. Most of the country had never heard of him until even a few weeks into the 2010 season. He was a fresh face and fresh story; he was hot off the presses. Secondly (strangely enough), he was awesome. Some consider Cam to be worthy of consideration as the greatest Auburn player of all time. It is too soon to make that judgment. One cannot deny, however, that Cam exhibited at times the Superman-type quality, meaning not just incredible skill and athleticism, but rather the seeming ability to do anything, that we most closely associate with Bo. I felt this way when I saw him add a receiving touchdown to his statistics against Ole Miss. The newness and awesomeness of Cam Newton were frequently expressed together in statements along the lines of "some thought he could be good, but nobody knew he would be like this." On top of these first two qualities was added Cam's charisma. His smile garnered as much attention as his running or passing. As our season gained momentum, Cam's post-game celebrations became more-and-more excited. He deeply reveled in the joy and satisfaction of winning, seemingly oblivious to all the cameras, which, of course, makes for the best TV and photos of all. With Tebow we had some back story, and with each passing season his legend in the making developed before our eyes. There was a national understanding of who Tebow was, both on and off the field, and every jump pass was interpreted in light of this understanding. We did not have this kind of nationally shared conception of Cam, because, again, he was new.[22] But, the media had something, from their perspective, even better: scandal.

Scandal does not have to be based on anything real. In fact, that is part of its allure – the mystery of whether or not those stirring up the commotion are telling the whole truth, or any truth at all. As if all this were not enough, Cam topped it all by thriving in the face of scandal, and even feeding off his success despite it all, which, in turn, bolstered his already spotlight-stealing charisma. So, looking back, it is no surprise that so many members of the media never shut up about Cam. They make their living off the sensational, and it was

---

[22] Interestingly enough, in some regards Newton did everything in one year that Tebow did in four: captured the media's attention like no other player; amassed an enormous fan base with equally fervent devotion; won the Heisman Trophy; led his team to a BCS Championship.

just too easy to keep the ball that was the Cam Newton story and non-story bouncing back-and-forth: they would report on his awesome performance, then temper it with reports of allegations, and then bounce back to how great he played each week even as the slander continued, and this cycle continued through and beyond the BCS Championship Game.[23]

Obviously, Cam's impact on our 2010 season was considerable. Would we have won a BCS Championship without him? I know that we could have. We still would have had all the other talent that blocked for him, that carried the ball when the defense was focused on him, that caught his passes, and that stopped our opponents to put him back on the field. I cannot agree with the sentiment supposedly expressed by Nick Saban, that we would have won only four games without Cam.[24]

To many, Cam, with his big smile, is the face of our 2010 season. To be sure, the focus that his role will receive in the

---

[23] One of the more ridiculous moments in the media's obsession with the constructed scandal regarding Cam was ESPN's Heisman Trophy Awards Show. I understand if they felt it would be disingenuous to say nothing about it that night after they had talked about it so much over the preceding months, but, there was no need to repeatedly bring it up, given that everyone watching (excepting bammers) had already seen/heard/read everything about it they could have possibly desired. Nonetheless, ESPN devoted so much attention to the non-story throughout the show that the "Cam Newton Scandal" may as well have been a fifth finalist for the award.

[24] I wonder what other 3 teams he thinks we would have beaten. Erick Smith, "Nick Saban: Auburn would have won four games without Cam Newton," n.p. [cited May 29, 2011]. Online: http://content.usatoday.com/communities/campusrivalry/post/20 11/04/alabama-nick-saban-auburn-four-wins-cam-newton/1?csp=34.

telling and re-telling of those 14 victories and the ascent to the highest point of football glory that they comprise is well deserved. At the same time, Cam took the stage in only the final act of the drama that was our journey from the dark place of 2008 to the bright fields of 2010. We would be remiss not to appropriately commend those who persevered through the trials of 2008, those whose Auburn careers are made up of more than 14 wins.

The remarkable stories are as many as the names on the rosters. Never mind the distractions both on and off the field common to every player, Zac Etheridge overcame an injury which initially made the thought of him returning to football preposterous. I remember the first time I heard the name Lee Ziemba. A friend of mine who follows recruiting told me we had gotten an important commitment. Sometimes highly recruited players never see a down of action. Other times they go on to break the school record for consecutive starts. I must admit I was on Ziemba's case throughout 2008 and 2009. I joked that he must be our all-time leader in false start yardage. Of course, nobody stops the game and makes an announcement to the whole stadium and TV audience when an offensive lineman opens up a hole for touchdown. In 2010, along with Mike Berry, A. J. Greene, Byron Isom, Brandon Mosley, and Ryan Pugh, Ziemba played on what may have been Auburn's greatest offensive line ever.

In 2007, when we saw Wes Byrum hit two winning field goals in one game on a Saturday night in Gainesville, no one imagined he would ever have anything from which to bounce back. But, fighting an injury and all the distractions of 2008, Byrum's field goal percentage dropped from 73.9 to 57.9. Byrum's cumulative percentage for 2009 and 2010 was 83.3, and when he was called on at the end of the BCS Championship Game – and no field goal is too short to miss – Byrum made arguably the biggest kick in our program's history.

Is there any other player whose Auburn career well represents the journey from the darkness of 2008 to the magnificence of 2010? Wait – this reminds me of a story . . .

I purchased our tickets for the 2008 game at Oxford prior to the start of the season. Pre-season expectations for the Rebels were high,[25] and I thought it likely we would be undefeated at that point in the season, so I thought it might be a highly anticipated game, and, thus, a tough ticket. It was not. Having lost to LSU, Vanderbilt, Arkansas, and having been stomped by West Virginia,[26] we traveled to Mississippi with as little confidence as I have ever taken on the road. Our seats were pretty low, behind the Auburn bench, at about the spot where our offense began our first possession of the game. Somehow my relatively up-close view of those navy jerseys[27] taking the field, led by no. 18, Kodi Burns, caused me to think, Oh yeah, we're Auburn – we can win this game. Though we did not, the point is that Kodi Burns was there.

Looking back, I do not know whether Kodi grew as much as one might be tempted to think during his time at Auburn. What I mean is the way he responded to the challenges of 2007 and all the more so of 2008 showed that he already possessed the poise and confidence of a leader. We may not have seen it so clearly until the meeting room speech of 2009, but, in retrospect, we can see it in the plays he ran in 2007, and even just in that moment when our offense took the field in Oxford in 2008.

---

[25] Proving sportswriters have a sense of humor.

[26] One might argue the Tennessee game should be counted as a lost. More than winning it felt like we lost a contest of who could look worse.

[27] Ole Miss, I suppose from some desire to pay homage to LSU, chose to wear white at home for this game.

Kodi Burns' career at Auburn makes for quite a story. We saw his talent in 2007, but we did not appear to know the best way to utilize it – at least not until New Year's Eve. After that night, hopes were very high. A thorough exploration of Tuberville's decision to hire Tony Franklin is beyond the scope of this work,[28] and yet, from the right angle it seemed to make sense: it looked as though in the college football world one could either get on the spread-offense train or be left behind, and Franklin had been successful at Troy. That night at the Georgia Dome, Tuberville's decision looked to be a stroke of managerial genius. But, then things got complicated.

In 2008, we, the fans, never really knew who the quarterback was, and, whenever the coaches told us who it was, we had trouble believing them, regardless of who they said. In the middle of all this was Kodi Burns,[29] but the confusion and frustration was demonstrated only by the coaches and fans. Still, would anyone have been very surprised if Burns had transferred after 2008? It would have made little practical sense, but we must imagine it could have felt like the right thing to do – to just take off and try again somewhere else.

---

[28] And probably any work.

[29] To be sure, also in the middle of it all was Chris Todd. Todd's story deserves as much attention as anyone's, and perhaps he will take opportunity at some point to tell it in full. The first 5 games of 2009 were incredibly exciting. As Chizik's (and Malzahn's) first quarterback at Auburn, Todd played an essential role in the administration's startup. It might sound a little strange to say that Todd deserves some credit for the success of 2010, but one cannot deny that his character impacted the beginning of the Chizik era. Todd was a part of the momentum started in 2009 that fed into the success of 2010.

We know now that such a move is not at all consistent with Burn's character. Soon afterwards, he would impact the 2009 season in as great a way off the field as any other player would between the lines. Burn's 2009 pre-season speech has become legendary. We all have heard stories of division on a football team. Our team had some struggles in 2009, but without Burn's plea to his teammates to be a team and to focus on winning championships, 2009 might have just become another story of a team fighting against itself. His selflessness gave our team unity, without which we never would have witnessed the excitement of 2009's initial win streak. Of course, we should not ignore that Kodi also contributed on the field in 2009, with 6 touchdowns, 75 passing yards, 175 rushing yards, and 46 yards receiving.

What might we have expected from Kodi Burns in 2010? After Cam Newton was named the starting quarterback, we hoped it unlikely that we would need a designated wildcat QB. Our receiving corps included Darvin Adams, Emory Blake, and Terrell Zachery. Would there be a place for Burns? For a while it appeared there may not. Through the first 8 games of the season, Burns had yet to accumulate a total of 100 all-purpose yards, and had scored only 1 touchdown. Of course, statistics do not tell the whole story. Burns made blocks on big plays, and on little ones, too. While I did not return to Oxford in 2010, Kodi Burns did, again wearing navy. He did not lead our team onto the field that day in the same role as he did on November 1, 2008, but he did complete the pass to Cam Newton that I above said made it seem like Cam could anything. Curtis Luper described Burns' completion as having provided Cam with a "Heisman moment."[30] The pass was Kodi's only throwing touchdown of 2010, and his last completion as an Auburn Tiger, but it was not his last contribution.

---

[30] http://www.youtube.com/watch?v=kEee1z0Xio8

How should we properly perceive the significance of each of Burns' two catches on November 26, 2010 in Tuscaloosa? Had either of them been dropped, or if Burns had failed to get open on either play, we would have lost the game. Philip Lutzenkirchen made the catch for the go-ahead touchdown, and that reception deserves all the recognition we give it. Nonetheless, in order to understand the meaningfulness of Burns two catches, imagine a different scenario: what if Auburn had scored a touchdown on the last play of the game to win 6-5? Think about the status that reception would hold in the legend of 2010. It would be something like if Courtney Taylor's 4th-down catch against LSU in 2004 had been against Alabama. That is the level of importance at which we should place each of Burns' two catches in Tuscaloosa. Take either of them away, and the 2010 BCS Champion would be Oregon or Boise State. On the topic of the BCS Championship, Burns only made one catch in Glendale, but it was good for 6 points, our team's first points of the game. For the Auburn Family, this was an inspiring moment: it was not an easy score, if there is such a thing – it was not a wide-open catch in the end zone or a sweep play with all the defenders going the wrong way. Instead, Burns made the catch and then ran like he was a playing for a championship, like he knew this was his opportunity to make his last highlight a part of a BCS Championship win.

10

ROYAL PSALMS

One of the many ways in which our community differs from that of the ancient Israelites is our lack of monarchy. Given the role of the king in the life of ancient Israel, it is not surprising that the Psalter contains a number of psalms pertaining to the life of the king. These psalms may contain a variety of elements: prayers for the king; praise of the king; and, even charges to the king regarding how he should rule. The identity of the community was closely bound up with the character and success (at home and abroad) of the king. Accordingly, the king was something of a champion of the people, just as the Auburn Tigers are the champions for the Auburn Family.

In 2010, our team became champions in another sense, namely, the champions of both the Southeastern Conference and also the Bowl Championship Series. This chapter will reflect upon winning those championship by focusing on Psalms 20 and 144.

Psalm 20

For the director of music. A psalm of David.

[1] May the LORD answer you when you are in distress;
  may the name of the God of Jacob protect you.
[2] May he send you help from the sanctuary
  and grant you support from Zion.
[3] May he remember all your sacrifices
  and accept your burnt offerings.
  Selah

[4] May he give you the desire of your heart
  and make all your plans succeed.
[5] We will shout for joy when you are victorious
  and will lift up our banners in the name of our God.
May the LORD grant all your requests.

[6] Now I know that the LORD saves his anointed;
  he answers him from his holy heaven
  with the saving power of his right hand.
[7] Some trust in chariots and some in horses,
  but we trust in the name of the LORD our God.
[8] They are brought to their knees and fall,
  but we rise up and stand firm.

[9] O LORD, save the king!
  Answer us when we call!

(vv. 1-5) Psalm 20 is a prayer spoken in a blessing formula by the community offered up to God on behalf of their earthly king. It is easy to see here correlations to prayers we might have prayed for our team during the final stretch of the 2010 season and post-season. Of course, the hope of v. 1 that the king be saved from distress was realized when our team rallied from being down 24 points. Verse 2 acknowledges the importance of help from home when traveling, and our team ventured to 3 different locations for the final three games of the 2010 campaign, always taking the support of the Auburn Family with them. Like the psalmist in vv. 3 and 4, we hoped that the preparations made by our team would prove efficacious for their mission, and that they would be granted the desire of their heart, namely SEC and BCS Championships. Regarding v. 5, we indeed shouted "War Eagle" for joy in response to our team's victory, already with our "banners high."

(vv. 6-8) In these verses this psalm seems to exhibit a characteristic sometimes found in laments, that being that we may be missing some information. Why is it that now the speaker knows "that the Lord saves his anointed?" Perhaps there was some report of victory that the psalmist could assume the community to be aware of apart from the psalm. Our first report of victory after Tuscaloosa came from Atlanta. If we were to imagine that the missing information between vv. 5 and 6 is the report of some particular, momentous event of such fame that it need not even be expressly recorded, then our equivalent conception might be the Hail Mary from Cam Newton to Darvin Adams at the end of the first half of the 2010 SEC Championship Game. That was a heck of a moment. South Carolina had scored, seemingly giving themselves some momentum going into the half and setting the stage for them to compete in the second half. Even after two full seasons of seeing Chizik and Malzahn at work, Auburn fans had previously been so accustomed to seeing our coaches let the air out of the ball whenever it seemed even remotely justifiable, that it was still a little surprising to see us come onto the field for our last possession of the first half with the apparent intent to score. Cam Newton, of course, in all aspects was built to play football, and one particular element of that is the notable applicability of his skills set to the Hail Mary – buy time;

heave the ball half a mile. It was fun to watch him do it. It would have been even if the ball had just been tipped a couple of times and then fallen uneventfully to the ground. When Darvin Adams made the type of play off the deflection that every receiver works so hard to be able to do and dreams of getting the chance to do, he turned what would have been just another play into something awesome. After that play, I could not help but think back to an attempted Hail Mary in 2009. On that day, our players gave it everything they had, right down to the last second. They earned our respect, admiration, and celebration no less than the 2010 team. The only difference was that, in the Georgia Dome on December 4, 2010, God was simply smiling on us in a different way. The pain on Spurrier's face as he left the field for half time showed he knew that, in 2010, our team just could not be beat. Verses 7-8 emphasize that anything on which people might place their trust other than "the name of the Lord our God" is definitively unreliable, but that those who trust in God will "rise up and stand firm." Anyone who really knows college football knows that winning an SEC Championship indeed constitutes standing firm. In 2004, we stood amidst a nasty storm of systemic insufficiency and media bias, but because we were undefeated, and also the champions of the best football conference in America, we stood firm. In 2011, the situation was even better, for we stood firm at the top of the BCS rankings, knowing we finally had the opportunity to play for college football's most widely recognized championship.

(v. 9) Psalm 20 concludes by restating the dependency of the people and the king upon the Lord. It indicates that though vv. 6-8 acknowledge some deliverance by the Lord, it will not be the last time the people and the king need the Lord to answer their plea for help. Of course, Atlanta was not the last stop on our team's journey, and we prayed for God's favor for one more game.

READING THE PSALMS AS AN AUBURN FAN

Psalm 144

Of David.

[1] Praise be to the LORD my Rock,
   who trains my hands for war,
   my fingers for battle.
[2] He is my loving God and my fortress,
   my stronghold and my deliverer,
my shield, in whom I take refuge,
   who subdues peoples under me.

[3] O LORD, what is man that you care for him,
   the son of man that you think of him?
[4] Man is like a breath;
   his days are like a fleeting shadow.

[5] Part your heavens, O LORD, and come down;
   touch the mountains, so that they smoke.
[6] Send forth lightning and scatter the enemies;
   shoot your arrows and rout them.
[7] Reach down your hand from on high;
   deliver me and rescue me
from the mighty waters,
   from the hands of foreigners
[8] whose mouths are full of lies,
   whose right hands are deceitful.

[9] I will sing a new song to you, O God;
   on the ten-stringed lyre I will make music to you,
[10] to the One who gives victory to kings,
   who delivers his servant David from the deadly sword.

[11] Deliver me and rescue me
   from the hands of foreigners

whose mouths are full of lies,
  whose right hands are deceitful.

¹² Then our sons in their youth
  will be like well-nurtured plants,
and our daughters will be like pillars
  carved to adorn a palace.
¹³ Our barns will be filled
  with every kind of provision.
Our sheep will increase by thousands,
  by tens of thousands in our fields;
¹⁴ our oxen will draw heavy loads.
There will be no breaching of walls,
  no going into captivity,
  no cry of distress in our streets.

¹⁵ Blessed are the people of whom this is true;
  blessed are the people whose God is the LORD.

(vv. 1-2) As we waited through most of December and the first 10 days of January, we certainly had reason to praise the Lord for having trained our hands for battle and our fingers for war. Otherwise, we never would have won 13 victories between September 4th and December 4th. Were God not our fortress, stronghold, deliverer, and shield, we surely would have fallen once, if not many times.

(vv. 3-4) The psalmist questions why God would even bother with mortal man. This question received our attention in ch. 2. Our days are, indeed, "like a fleeting shadow," and a single football season passes with a snap of the fingers. We would be wise to celebrate our BCS Championship every single day. I do not mean to say that we will not win one again, but putting together the kind of season it requires is a special thing, and we would be foolish not to savor each moment while we are on top of the football world.

(vv. 5-8) Here the speaker contemplates the magnificence that is God's intervention in his creation. It is an incredible display when the Creator of all things reaches down his hand from on high. The challenges faced by our team were as formidable as mighty waters, our opponents as fierce as deceitful foreigners.

(vv. 9-10) The reminder of this psalm expresses hope for the type of blessings we experienced in winning the BCS Championship. Our team's accomplishments inspired a number of new songs,[31] and gave us a new voice for our old ones. God is "the one who gives victory to kings," and he has made Auburn the King of College Football.

(v. 11) Our prayer for deliverance was answered in November. This supposition may have been included here in the psalm as an acknowledgement of the speaker's continued dependence upon God.

(vv. 12-14) The penultimate section of Psalm 144 expresses a variety of the impacts of divine favor. Our children inherit the glory of Auburn's 2010 BCS Championship. Only 11 programs have won a BCS Championship, and our children can claim a regal place for our program that most cannot.

(vv. 13-14) Our barns were "filled with every kind of provision". In addition to the trophies for the SEC and BCS Championships, Auburn players and coaches won the following awards: The Heisman Trophy, Manning Award, Maxwell Award, Walter Camp Award, Davey O'Brien Award (Cam Newton); The Lombardi Award (Nick Fairley); The Frank Broyles Award (Gus Malzahn); the Home Depot Coach of the Year (Gene Chizik). Ryan Pugh was also a

---

[31] e.g. Orange Navy
http://www.youtube.com/watch?v=PH6r2lmsb0I

finalist for both the Rimington Trophy and the Lowe's Senior Class Award. The 2010 Auburn Tigers, like the Auburn Spirit, will never be defeated. Those who hope for the breaching of our walls have already seen their finest hour. We will not go into captivity, but the crystal ball on display in The Rane Room at the Auburn Athletic Complex will captivate Auburn Fans always.

(v. 15) The Hebrew word here translated "blessed" is אשרי. The precise meaning of this word is a matter of some debate among Old Testament scholars. Our understanding of it can benefit from observing its use in Ps 65:4: "Blessed are those you choose and bring near to live in your courts!" It is because we were chosen by God, and not by our own merits, that we, the Auburn Family, experienced and still enjoy the incredible 2010 season. This reality was best expressed by Gene Chizik at the January 22, 2011 BCS Championship Celebration at Jordan-Hare Stadium: "God said 'Yes' to Auburn Football.

11

BUT, WHAT ABOUT OUR TREES?

It is a difficult question. If our winning a BCS Championship somehow resulted from the beneficence of a just God, how could that same God allow our year of celebration to be interrupted by an apparent death blow to one of the oldest symbols of what it means to be an Auburn Tiger? Like all Auburn fans, I experienced a variety of disquieting emotions upon hearing the news: sadness, anger, confusion, even despair. In the darkest moment of my contemplation, I felt our enemies had managed to get the last laugh – there was no sense in writing a book that at all depicted God as showing favor to the Auburn Family. The passage of time, however, provided wider perspective. First of all, if we believe in the God of the Bible, we need not concern ourselves with any possibility that the perpetrator was acting in a way that could please God. The poisoning of the Toomers' Oaks was not just a crime against the Auburn Family as well as against the environment. Rather, it was an attack against God's creation. To poison tress that God has seen fit to keep alive for better than 125 years is to look at what God has called good and say, "not good." The most cursory examination of the Psalter will find support therein for this fact, as the very first image employed by the psalmists is arboreal in nature: Ps 1:3: "He is like a tree planted by streams of water, which yields its fruit in season and whose leaf does not wither. Whatever he does prospers."

The Psalms as a whole also help us accept this tragedy. As was discussed in ch. 4, the psalmists' enemies and the wicked are present virtually throughout the Psalter. Whenever the psalmists give thanks for deliverance from their enemies, it is never long before they appear again. This is simply a reality of the corrupted world in which we presently live. For this short moment (meaning human history since The Fall) in God's eternal plan, evil is allowed to exists on the earth. It will always be here, regularly raising its sinful head with sometimes more deplorable results than others, until Christ Jesus returns in Judgment over all creation. Accordingly, even in an instance like this, we should not be surprised to see the persistence of evil in this world.

Of course, the poisoning of the trees is connected to a principle already covered above – previously our enemies knew they could not beat us on the field, and so they attacked us elsewhere. After the unsuccessful smear campaign against the Auburn Family with regards to Cam Newton, we would have been wise to be on guard for something else, especially after the way our team humiliated our rivals by winning even after spotting them a 24-point lead. We should have known that some representative of those who wish us harm would be out for their pound of flesh. I know it is easy for me to say this in hindsight, and, I assure you, it had not occurred to me before the news of the poisoning broke that our threat level should have been raised. At the same time, I have no idea what it would have cost to provide adequate 24/7 security for every possible target of retaliation for the comeback.

What I do know is that the response of the Auburn Family to this event and the Spirit of solidarity and hope and all the ideas expressed in the Creed are more important than the Oaks themselves. At the same time, while we have been told to expect the trees to die, they are not dead yet, and we have also been told that the University is proceeding as if we have a chance to save them. I enjoy imagining a day when it is announced that the efforts to save the trees have been successful, that they may always remind of us of Ps 104:16: "The trees of the LORD are well watered, the cedars of Lebanon that he planted."

12

CONCLUSION

The Psalter is a book about faith. It expresses the foundation and function of the faith of the ancient Israelite community. The Psalms also deal head-on, arguably in a way found nowhere else in Scripture, with the challenge of reconciling faith and the sometimes troubling events of daily life. The life of a football fan is one of faith. When a fan joins his or her identity to that of a team or program, he or she is acting in faith that that team or program will conduct itself in such a way that the fan can say with conviction, "That is my team." There are a variety of ways of living out this faith. Sometimes it means making sacrifices in order to attend a game. Other times it means affirming one's allegiance to his or her team on Friday, and still coming into work on Monday. This faith sometimes takes the form of proudly wearing one's colors in the student section of the opposing team. On other days, it means going to the mall, grocery store, hardware store, etc. wearing apparel that advertises one's allegiance, even when it is difficult to be proud of his or her team's performance.

Many Auburn fans maintain, or at least at some point have maintained, dual citizenship – they live in both the Bible Belt and the Southeastern Conference. And, of course, even

Auburn Fans who have never lived in the South understand something of the implications of living in these coexisting regions, and sometimes those implications are experienced just as vividly in other parts of the country, as well as the globe.

My observation has been that many fans of various programs, even, or especially, while living in these geographically identical but sociologically differentiated realms prefer, in some regard, to live in one on Saturday, another on Sunday,[32] and then some mixture of the two on Monday. One of my objectives for this book was to confront the concept that someone who is deeply devoted to both their faith and their football keeps the two separated in any real way. Granted, this may be the case entirely for some individuals. My experience, however, has shown me that many who claim to maintain such a distinction, do not reflect the separation in their words or actions. One possible explanation for why Christian football fans even bother to claim that their theological beliefs and sports enthusiasm are not intertwined is that many Southerners do not perceive religion as a sociological phenomenon. For some, religion, or spirituality, is a uniquely distinct entity, containing ultimate truth, far above the observations and theories that derive from the study of human, cultural phenomena. Let the reader understand – I, too, believe that the death and resurrection of Christ Jesus, and the fact that therein lies the only way to be reconciled to God the Father, is more real than anything else in this world. I also recognize that we presently live in a physical world inhabited by mortal man, and that just as the

---

[32] I am using the term *Sunday* here very figuratively, as, of course, as much or more bragging or bickering about football takes place at church as anywhere else. By *Sunday* I mean one's theological perspective and expressed beliefs. This *Sunday* might be an actual Sunday in the heart of basketball season (this was more true before the common fan was so interested in recruiting).

physical sciences provide us with useable knowledge to make possible technological advancements, so do the human sciences provide us with knowledge that makes possible better understanding of our own behavior. Accordingly, while the Christian religion contains ultimate truth, it is still a religion, and it still operates in our earthly lives as a sociological phenomenon. For this reason, it cannot operate in a vacuum, untouched by the other sociological phenomena that impact our lives. For many fans, football and faith are very clearly among the most influential determinants in how we relate to each other and in how we respond to all the various events that, in some regard, constitute living in society, or even just living on this planet.

My belief in and observation of the intertwining of these two influences is what enable me to read the Psalms as an Auburn Fan and to look back on the 2009 and 2010 football seasons through the lens of the Psalter. Having made the journey outlined in the previous chapters from November 2008 to January 2011 raises an obvious question: what if the future appears to bring disappointment with regards to our correlation between reading the Psalms and winning the BCS Championship? The first thing we must say in answering this question is that the future almost certainly will bring disappointment, at least relative to 2010. I will not deny the possibility that our players and coaches can accomplish everything in 2011 that was accomplished in 2010. As fans, however, we must understand that right now we are in the one position that is more difficult to hold than any other – the very top.

The always recurring appearance of the enemies and the wicked, as well as other reasons for lamentation in the Psalter testify to the reality that this world will never be continually idyllic. If apparent injustice occurs in the future, we would be wise not to view it as some negation of 2010, but rather to remember that the God who blessed us in 2010 is still in control. Should we face disquieting times in the future, we must remember that the 1970s were followed by the 1980s, 1992 was overcome by 1993, and 2009 was eclipsed by 2010. It's Great to Be an Auburn Tiger!

T. C. NOMEL

Psalm 100

A psalm. For giving thanks.

[1] Shout for joy to the LORD, all the earth.
[2] Worship the LORD with gladness;
come before him with joyful songs.
[3] Know that the LORD is God.
It is he who made us, and we are his;
we are his people, the sheep of his pasture.

[4] Enter his gates with thanksgiving
and his courts with praise;
give thanks to him and praise his name.
[5] For the LORD is good and his love endures forever;
his faithfulness continues through all generations.

READING THE PSALMS AS AN AUBURN FAN

The Auburn Creed

I believe that this is a practical world and that I can count only on what I earn.

Therefore, I believe in work, hard work.

I believe in education, which gives me the knowledge to work wisely and trains my mind and my hands to work skillfully.

I believe in honesty and truthfulness, without which I cannot win the respect and confidence of my fellow men.

I believe in a sound mind, in a sound body and a spirit that is not afraid, and in clean sports that develop these qualities.

I believe in obedience to law because it protects the rights of all.

I believe in the human touch, which cultivates sympathy with my fellow men and mutual helpfulness and brings happiness for all.

I believe in my Country, because it is a land of freedom and because it is my own home, and that I can best serve that country by "doing justly, loving mercy, and walking humbly with my God."

And because Auburn men and women believe in these things, I believe in Auburn and love it.

-George Petrie

Appendix A: Youtube summaries

Because the youtube videos referred to in this book could vanish at any moment, they are below summarized for future reference. The numbers listed correspond to the footnotes in which the youtube url is cited.

7. "Auburn Tiges Pat Dye talking to Players" – Pat Dye addresses his players in the locker room after a loss at Knoxville in 1981.

15. "Alabama Crimson Tide quarterback Greg McElroy body slammed and knocked out in Iron Bowl 2010" – Bell repeatedly throws McElroy to the ground, set to the music *Bodies* by Drowning Pool.

20. "Cam Newton's musical welcome to Iron Bowl" – the team takes the field in Tuscaloosa for the pre-game look around.

21. "SCAM NEWTON.mp4" – WVUA News at Ten, in a video uploaded Nov 10, 2010, reports on the selling of *$camNewton Tees* at Alabama Express, a store in Tuscaloosa.

30. "AU Football: Every Day... Kodi's TD Throw to Cam vs. Ole Miss (Ep. 9)" – multiple players and coaches discuss Newton's touchdown pass to Kodi Burns.

31. "Young ie- Orange Navy (AUBURN EDITION)" – R&B artist Young IE presents his revision of Wiz Khalifa's "Black and Yellow."

Appendix B: Schedules and Results

2008

Aug. 30	Louisiana-Monroe	W	34-0
Sep. 6	Southern Miss	W	27-13
Sep. 13	at Mississippi State	W	3-2
Sep. 20	LSU	L	26-21
Sep. 27	Tennessee	W	14-12
Oct. 4	at Vanderbilt	L	14-13
Oct. 11	Arkansas	L	25-22
Oct. 23	at West Virginia	L	34-17
Nov. 1	at Ole Miss	L	17-7
Nov. 8	Tennessee-Martin	W	37-20
Nov. 15	Georgia	L	17-13
Nov. 29	at UAT	L	36-0

2009

Sep. 5	La. Tech	W	37-13
Sep. 12	Mississippi State	W	49-24
Sep. 19	West Virginia	W	41-30
Sep. 26	Ball State	W	54-30
Oct. 3	at Tennessee	W	26-22
Oct. 10	at Arkansas	L	44-23
Oct. 17	Kentucky	L	21-14
Oct. 24	at LSU	L	31-10
Oct. 31	Ole Miss	W	33-20
Nov. 7	Furman	W	63-31
Nov. 14	at Georgia	L	31-24
Nov. 27	UAT	L	26-21

<u>Outback Bowl</u>

Jan. 1, 2010	Northwestern	W	38-35

2010

Sep. 4	Arkansas State	W	52-26
Sep. 9	at Mississippi State	W	17-14
Sep. 18	Clemson	W	27-24
Sep. 25	South Carolina	W	35-27
Oct. 2	Louisiana-Monroe	W	52-3
Oct. 9	at Kentucky	W	37-34
Oct. 16	Arkansas	W	65-43
Oct. 23	LSU	W	24-17
Oct. 30	at Ole Miss	W	51-31
Nov. 6	UTC	W	62-24
Nov. 13	Georgia	W	49-31
Nov. 26	at UAT	W	28-27

SEC Championship

Dec. 4	South Carolina	W	56-17

BCS Championship

Jan. 10, 2011	Oregon	W	22-19

2011

Sep. 3   Utah State

Sep. 10   Mississippi State

Sep. 17   at Clemson

Sep. 24   Florida Atlantic

Oct. 1   at South Carolina

Oct. 8   at Arkansas

Oct. 15   Florida

Oct. 22   at LSU

Oct. 29   Ole Miss

Nov. 12   at Georgia

Nov. 19   Samford

Nov. 26   UAT

<u>SEC Championship</u>

Dec. 3   TBD